199
Facts About
Being a U.S. Citizen

By Jessica E. Piper

I DIDN'T LEARN THAT IN HIGH SCHOOL: 199 FACTS ABOUT BEING A U.S. CITIZEN

1405 SW 6th Avenue • Ocala, Florida 34471 • Phone 800-814-1132 • Fax 352-622-1875
Website: www.atlantic-pub.com • Email: sales@atlantic-pub.com
SAN Number: 268-1250

Library of Congress Cataloging-in-Publication Data

Names: Piper, Jessica E., 1994- author.
Title: I didn't learn that in high school : 199 facts about being a U .S. citizen / by Jessica E. Piper.
Description: Ocala, Florida : Atlantic Publishing Group, Inc., [2017] | Includes bibliographical references and index.
Identifiers: LCCN 2017019199 (print) | LCCN 2017032768 (ebook) | ISBN 9781620231760 (ebook) | ISBN 9781620231753 (alk. paper) | ISBN 1620231751 (alk. paper)
Subjects: LCSH: Citizenship—United States.
Classification: LCC JK1759 (ebook) | LCC JK1759 .P48 2017 (print) | DDC 323.60973—dc23
LC record available at https://lccn.loc.gov/2017019199

Printed in the United States

PROJECT MANAGER: Lisa McGinnes • lmcginnes@atlantic-pub.com
INTERIOR LAYOUT: Nicole Sturk • nicolejonessturk@gmail.com

Reduce. Reuse.
RECYCLE.

A decade ago, Atlantic Publishing signed the Green Press Initiative. These guidelines promote environmentally friendly practices, such as using recycled stock and vegetable-based inks, avoiding waste, choosing energy-efficient resources, and promoting a no-pulping policy. We now use 100-percent recycled stock on all our books. The results: in one year, switching to post-consumer recycled stock saved 24 mature trees, 5,000 gallons of water, the equivalent of the total energy used for one home in a year, and the equivalent of the greenhouse gases from one car driven for a year.

Over the years, we have adopted a number of dogs from rescues and shelters. First there was Bear and after he passed, Ginger and Scout. Now, we have Kira, another rescue. They have brought immense joy and love not just into our lives, but into the lives of all who met them.

We want you to know a portion of the profits of this book will be donated in Bear, Ginger and Scout's memory to local animal shelters, parks, conservation organizations, and other individuals and nonprofit organizations in need of assistance.

– Douglas & Sherri Brown,
President & Vice-President of Atlantic Publishing

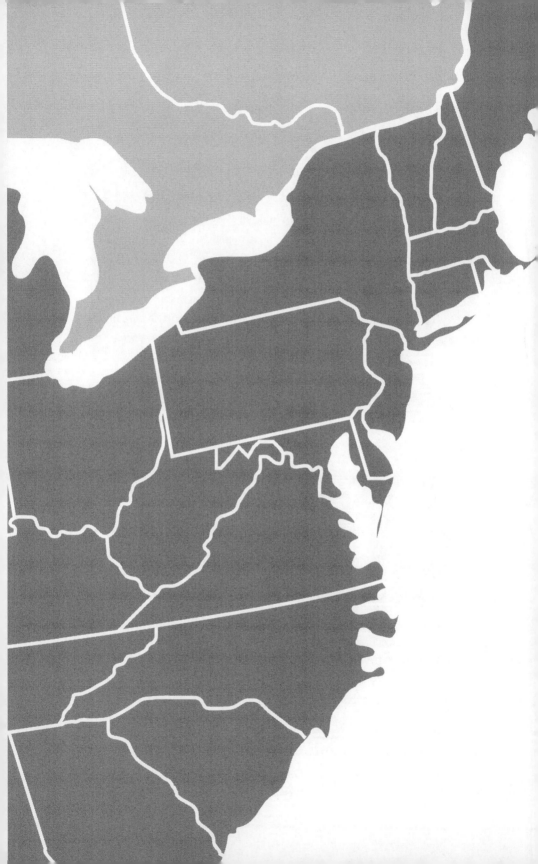

Table of Contents

Introduction

I f you are born a U.S. citizen, you might not think much about what it means to be one. Being a citizen of the United States gives enormous privileges — for example, the right to live and work in a free country, the opportunity to vote in elections and run for public office, and the freedom to travel nearly anywhere in the world.

Perhaps the value of U.S. citizenship is best shown by the efforts some people put in to obtain it. Every year, millions of people apply for U.S. visas with the hope of immigrating and someday obtaining permanent residency. Not everyone is successful — many encounter long wait lists and must re-apply several times; those who are lucky enough to get a visa must pay fees, fill out paperwork, and ultimately leave their home countries to settle in the United States. Once they arrive, they must adjust to a new culture, sometimes without the comfort of their friends or family. After a certain amount of time, they become eligible for U.S. citizenship — but only if they fill out more paperwork, undergo a background check, take tests about American government and the English language, complete an interview, and formally swear their allegiance to the United States.

This book will discuss what it means to be a U.S. citizen. It will give an overview of the citizenship process, from acquiring a visa to completing naturalization. It will also provide basic insight into American history, government, and the Constitution, so that individuals applying for citizenship can learn the necessary material to pass their exam, and people who already are U.S. citizens can refresh their own knowledge and learn what is expected of new members of the country.

U.S. citizenship isn't simple. In fact, the laws around immigration and citizenship are incredibly complicated and nuanced, with many categories and exceptions. Nonetheless, the 199 facts in this book will provide insight into the many ways individuals become U.S. citizens, as well as the history of citizenship and the rights and responsibilities of all citizens today. Are you ready to dive into the fundamental definition of being an American? Keep reading.

CHAPTER 1

What Makes a Citizen?

A baby boy is born to immigrant parents in Los Angeles. An Iranian-born woman takes the Oath of Allegiance at a naturalization ceremony in New York City. A girl grows up in Germany where her American parents moved before she was born. These three individuals may not seem to have much in common, but they have one major similarity—they are all U.S. citizens.

There are several different pathways to U.S. citizenship. Many people are born U.S. citizens, while some acquire citizenship through naturalization—a legal process where applicants fill out forms, undergo several tests, and ultimately swear their allegiance to the United States. For the most part, the laws about who is or can become a citizen are simple, but certain citizenship cases are complicated. This chapter will address who is automatically a U.S. citizen and how a person can become one.

CITIZEN BY BIRTH

Today, the United States follows a principle known as birthright citizenship—individuals born within the boundaries of the country are automatically citizens. This means that children born in any hospital in the United States are citizens from the moment they come into the world, regardless of the citizenship of their parents.

Fact #I

★ ☆ ★

Generally, a child is born a U.S. citizen if they are born on U.S. soil, including the 50 states and most U.S. territories, or if either of their parents is a U.S. citizen.

In addition to birthright citizenship, U.S. law dictates than children born abroad to U.S. parents are usually citizens as well. This provision makes sense, particularly in an era where international travel is fairly easy. For example, if an American woman on vacation delivers her child in another country, she won't have to fight to make that child a U.S. citizen.

Not so simple

Automatic citizenship for children born in the U.S. and born abroad to U.S. citizen parents seems like a fairly simple rule. However, there are a few complications to these rules. First, there is a small exception to the birth-right citizenship rule. Most foreign countries have embassies with diplomats who live in the United States. The children of these diplomats become citizens of their parents' home country, even if they are born on U.S. soil.

Fact #2
★ ☆ ★

Children of foreign diplomats born in the United States are not American citizens, and children born abroad to U.S. citizen parents may not be citizens if their parents have not lived in the United States.

This particular law seems like common sense. If a French ambassador working in Washington D.C. delivers a child, she probably wants her child to be a citizen of France, not the United States.

About those parents

There are also a few regulations on the citizenship of children born abroad to U.S. citizen parents. These children may not be citizens if their parents have not lived in the United States since childhood, but the laws also vary depending on which parent is a U.S. citizen. If both of the parents are U.S. citizens, the child is a citizen so long as one of the parents lived in the United States at any time prior to the child's birth.

If the parents are married and only one parent is a U.S. citizen, then the U.S. citizen parent must have lived in the United States for at least two years after the age of 14 and five years total for the child to be granted U.S. citizenship at birth. If the child's parents are unmarried and only one is a U.S. citizen, the child may still be granted citizenship, but the requirements become even more complicated. Additionally, if only the father is a U.S. citizen, the family may have to provide biological proof of fatherhood so that the child is recognized as a citizen.

What counts as the U.S.?

An additional complication to the question of birthright citizenship is how to define U.S. soil. When the United States was founded, the country included just 13 states; now it includes 50. Additionally, the United States has several overseas territories. While these territories are governed differently than the 50 states, they are still part of the country.

Fact #3

While people born in most U.S. territories are U.S. citizens, individuals born in American Samoa are considered U.S. nationals, not U.S. citizens.

In the early 1900s, a series of court cases known as the "Insular Cases" ruled that overseas U.S. possessions were considered "unincorporated territories." As a result, people who lived in these territories were not entitled to U.S. citizenship. These territories include Guam, the U.S. Virgin Islands, the Northern Mariana Islands, Puerto Rico, and American Samoa. In all of those territories except American Samoa, laws since then have overruled the court and granted citizenship to residents. People born in American Samoa, however, are considered U.S. nationals, not U.S. citizens. Even if they move to the U.S. mainland, they are not allowed to vote in elections or run for public office.

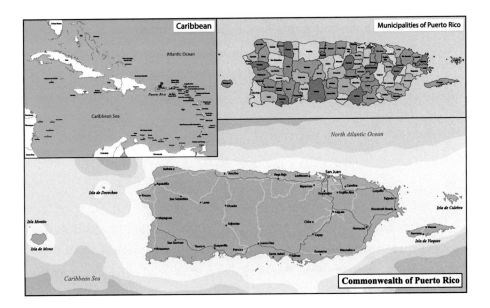

Proving citizenship

Given the many benefits of U.S. citizenship, people must have a way to prove that they are U.S. citizens. Since birth certificates indicate place of birth, anyone born in the United States can use their birth certificate as proof of citizenship.

Individuals born abroad who qualify as U.S. citizens can obtain their proof of citizenship by filling out an N-600 form, which is an application for a Certificate of Citizenship. In addition to completing this form, individuals must submit evidence—including birth and marriage certificates—to show that their parent was a U.S. citizen. There is also a $1,170 filing fee to submit an N-600 form.

NATURALIZATION

People who are not born U.S. citizens can acquire citizenship through a process known as naturalization. Only people already legally residing in the United States can apply for naturalization, and the process is not easy. Individuals must fill out forms, pay fees, face a background check, go through an interview, and take a citizenship test before they are granted the opportunity to swear their allegiance to the United States and become a U.S. citizen. The naturalization process will be discussed more thoroughly in Chapter 4.

Fact #4

★ ☆ ★

Naturalized citizens enjoy the same rights, privileges and duties as people who are born U.S. citizens, with a few small exceptions. For example, naturalized citizens are not allowed to become president—the Constitution specifies that the president must be a "natural born citizen."

Who's in charge of citizenship?

Most citizenship-related matters fall under the power of the United States Citizenship and Immigration Services (USCIS). USCIS processes most of the paperwork associated with applying for citizenship and administers citizenship tests.

Fact #5

★ ☆ ★

USCIS is a subset of the Department of Homeland Security (DHS).

In addition to citizenship, USCIS also deals with immigration. Immigration and citizenship are strongly connected—individuals who apply to be naturalized U.S. citizens are immigrants who once moved to the United States. Chapter 3 of this book with address the various ways that immigrants because U.S. permanent residents.

Fact #6

★ ☆ ★

USCIS manages many immigration-related services,
including the processing of asylum claims, the
administration of immigrant benefits, and the issuance
of employment authorization documents.

Permanent residency

The most common pathway to citizenship is through permanent residency. An individual who is a permanent resident has many of the same rights as a citizen—they can drive, hold a job, attend college, and travel outside the country. Unlike certain categories of immigrants, permanent residents are allowed to stay in the United States indefinitely. Their right to live in the country is not dependent on a job they hold or a school they attend.

Fact #7

★ ☆ ★

A U.S. permanent resident refers to anyone who lawfully
holds a green card.

However, permanent residents also have to deal with some barriers. Green cards—which provide proof that permanent residents are allowed to be in the United States—must be renewed every ten years, and sometimes more frequently. Currently, there is a $455 filing fee each time a permanent resident must renew. Additionally, permanent residents cannot vote in U.S.

elections, hold an elected office, or take many federal jobs. No matter how long they have lived in the United States, they are still at risk for deportation — removal from the country — if they commit certain crimes.

Fact #8

★ ☆ ★

An individual typically must be a U.S. permanent resident for five years before applying for naturalization.

Although there are a few exceptions, which will be discussed later in this book, most individuals who apply for U.S. citizenship are permanent residents who have been living in the country for at least five years.

Dual citizenship

Dual citizens are people who are citizens of two countries at the same time. Dual citizenship can occur automatically. For example, Canada, like the

United States, offers birthright citizenship. If a child is born in Canada to American parents, they will be a citizen of both countries.

Every country has its own laws concerning citizenship. While the United States allows for dual citizenship, not all countries do. In these cases, people may have to choose which country they would like to be a citizen of. People who are citizens of another country and are seeking to become naturalized U.S. citizens should check the laws of their native country to figure out if dual citizenship is allowed.

CASE STUDY

"I fully intended to maintain dual citizenship, but discovered after receiving US citizenship that the South African authorities required advance notice of such an intention in order to bestow dual citizenship. Now, I am supposed to tussle with another set of stooges, this time in South Africa, for 'permission' after the event."
                                                                          — Jonathan

In conclusion

As this chapter demonstrates, there are multiple ways people become U.S. citizens. Luckily, once someone becomes a citizen, how they did it hardly matters — U.S. citizens share numerous rights and privileges, regardless of whether they were born or naturalized. U.S. citizenship hasn't always been how it was today. The next chapter will address the history of citizenship, and how the rules about who can — and can't be — a citizen have changed during the course of American history.

CHAPTER 2

A History of Citizenship

The requirements for U.S. citizenship have changed dramatically over the course of American history. At times, the government passed laws to restrict who could become a citizen, often for political or racial reasons. Amendments to the Constitution redefined citizenship, and the Supreme Court was sometimes forced to interpret both the Constitution and other laws and decide who was actually a citizen.

In thinking about the meaning of being an American citizen, it is worthwhile to consider how the requirements for citizenship have changed over time. This chapter provides a brief history of citizenship in the United States.

CITIZENSHIP AND THE CONSTITUTION

The original American citizens were former subjects of the British Empire. When the United States declared itself independent from Great Britain in 1776, residents of the 13 states became citizens of a new nation. But from the very beginning, citizenship wasn't for everyone. Many of the Founding Fathers—who wrote the U.S. Constitution—were slave owners. They didn't want to grant citizenship to their slaves.

Fact #9
★ ☆ ★

Although the original U.S. Constitution mentioned the
rights of citizens, it gave no definition for who was a
citizen, or could become one.

While the Constitution sidestepped the definition of citizenship, the first
law to define who could become a citizenship in the United States was the
Naturalization Act of 1790. It declared that citizenship in the new nation
belonged only to a "white person" of "good moral character" who had lived
in the country for at least two years. This meant that African-Americans
and Native Americans were excluded from citizenship in the new nation.

Fact #10
★ ☆ ★

In the 1857 case *Dred Scott v. Sandford*, the Supreme
Court specifically ruled that black slaves were not
citizens, even though they were born in the
United States.

In 1857, an African-American slave named Dred Scott sued his master for
his freedom, based on the grounds that the pair had traveled to states where
slavery was illegal. Scott lost the suit. The Supreme Court didn't rule on
whether Scott's travels made him a free man, but instead argued that he
had no right to sue in the first place because he was not a U.S. citizen. The
Dred Scott v. Sandford reinforced that African-Americans were not considered citizens.

As it turned out, the United States would go to war over the issue of slavery just a few years after Scott's case. On the other side of the war, an

amendment to the Constitution would change the definition of American citizenship.

The 14th Amendment

The 14th Amendment to the Constitution was passed in 1868, three years after the end of the Civil War. The amendment has five sections which address a variety of issues pertaining to equal rights. It has been cited in many major court decisions, including *Brown v. Board of Education*, which ended official school segregation in 1954, and *Obergefell v. Hodges*, which legalized same-sex marriage in 2015.

The first section of the 14th Amendment addresses citizenship: "All persons born or naturalized in the United States, and subject to the jurisdiction thereof, are citizens of the United States and of the state wherein they reside."

Fact #11

★ ☆ ★

The 14th amendment established the principle of birthright citizenship—anyone born in the United States is automatically a citizen.

When it was passed, the 14th Amendment was intended to grant citizenship to former African-American slaves, who were freed after the war. By declaring that anyone born in the United States was a citizen, the 14th Amendment made sure that former slaves, who were almost universally born within the country, were citizens. As it turned out, the amendment would continue to play a role in U.S. history and would have implications not just for former slaves, but also for many other groups of Americans.

Fact #12

★ ☆ ★

Although the 14th amendment guaranteed citizenship
for all people born in the U.S., immigrants from certain
countries were still barred from applying for
citizenship. The Naturalization Act of 1870 declared
that only "white persons and persons of African
descent" could become naturalized citizens.

IMMIGRATION AND CITIZENSHIP

The United States is often regarded as a nation of immigrants. Some of the first settlers were Protestants fleeing religious persecution. Later immigrants to the colonies sought economic opportunities and hoped to create better lives for their families. Immigration did not stop after American independence. For example, many Irish moved across the ocean after their country was hit by a devastating potato famine in the 1840s, and large numbers of Germans immigrated to the United States in the 1850s.

Unlike present day, where immigrants must follow a rigorous process to legally move to the United States, it was pretty difficult for the government to keep track of who came into the country. As a result there were few formal regulations on immigration for most of the nineteen century.

Life wasn't always easy for the Irish, Germans, and other immigrants who settled in the United States in the 1800s. These new immigrants sometimes faced discrimination. Still, many saw moving to the United States an opportunity to start a new life, and they were willing to take their chances.

Chinese immigrants, new restrictions

Following the Civil War, a new immigrant group began emerging, this time on the West Coast. These new immigrants were directly tied to the massive economic growth taking place in the American West. In 1869, the transcontinental railroad was completed, connecting the state of California with the industrial centers on the East Coast. The railroads, and the economic growth that accompanied them, were strongly enabled by the efforts of immigrants. Railroad companies—in need of cheap labor—advertised in China, and thousands of Chinese men moved to California to work.

As the number of Chinese immigrants grew, many native-born Americans began to fear them. Violence sometimes broke out between Chinese immigrants and white Americans in cities like Los Angeles. When the economy worsened in the 1870s, people blamed Chinese workers. The Chinese were convenient scapegoats for all sorts of problems in California and the West.

The Chinese Exclusion Act

Fact #13
★ ☆ ★

The Chinese Exclusion Act of 1882 banned any Chinese nationals from being naturalized as U.S. citizens.

In response to popular sentiments about Chinese immigrants, President Chester A. Arthur signed the Chinese Exclusion Act in 1882. This law banned future Chinese immigrants from entering the country. With regards to citizenship, the law also declared that Chinese already living in the United States would carry out their lives as foreigners—they would never be eligible for naturalization, on account of their country of origin.

The Chinese Exclusion Act was the first law to ban certain groups from immigrating to the United States, and it would not be the last. In the late 1800s and early 1900s, several more laws were passed to restrict immigrants who were considered undesirable.

Citizenship laws and the Supreme Court

Given the laws about citizenship in the 1800s, there were many questions about who could really become a citizen. In several of these cases, the Supreme Court had to intervene and rule whether certain individuals were actually U.S. citizens.

Wong Kim Ark was born in San Francisco to Chinese immigrant parents who had immigrated legally to the United States before the passage of the Chinese Exclusion Act. In 1895, Ark tried to return to the United States after a trip to China, but he was denied entry on the basis that he was Chinese, and therefore could not immigrate to the United States.

Fact #14
★ ☆ ★

In 1898, the Supreme Court ruled in the case *United States v. Wong Kim Ark* that people born in the United States are U.S. citizens, regardless of their race or ethnicity.

Ark sued, and his case went all the way to the Supreme Court. In 1898, the Supreme Court ruled in Ark's favor. Based on the 14th Amendment, the decision said, Ark was a U.S. citizen because he was born in California. Birthright citizenship was extended to everyone, regardless of their race. Therefore, Ark could not be denied entry into the United States.

The Supreme Court's decision in *United States v. Wong Kim Ark* set an important precedent, and has been cited in many court cases since. Still, when Ark was officially recognized as a citizen in 1898, the United States still had a long way to go regarding citizenship.

Losing citizenship

During the early 1900s, several laws addressed how individuals could lose their U.S. citizenship. Passed in 1907, the Expatriation Act described several of the ways Americans could lose their citizenship: for example, by being naturalized a citizen of another nation, or taking an Oath of Allegiance to a country other than the United States. For women, however, there was an additional way to lose citizenship.

Fact #15

The Expatriation Act of 1907 declared that American women who married foreigners would lose their U.S. citizenship.

This provision of the Expatriation Act was unsurprisingly unpopular with many women, especially suffragists, who were in the midst of campaigning to get women the right to vote. After American women gained the right to vote in 1920, the Cable Act of 1922 declared that only women who married Asian men would lose their citizenship—women who married men of European descent could continue as U.S. citizens. This portion of the law was eventually repealed in 1931, allowing American woman to keep their U.S. citizenship, no matter whom they married.

So who is white?

Although the Supreme Court ruled that anyone born in the United States was a citizen regardless of race, laws still dictated that only white immigrants would be eligible for naturalization. These laws brought up an interesting question: What made an immigrant white? As it turned out, the Supreme Court would come up with that definition over the course of two court cases in the 1920s.

In 1922, a Japanese immigrant businessman named Takao Ozawa petitioned the Supreme Court for his naturalization. Because he was a Japanese citizen, U.S. law said that he couldn't apply to be naturalized. However, Ozawa argued to the court that he was culturally white. He had attended the University of California in Berkeley. His children were born in the United States. He attended church on Sundays, and—he told the court—he was a loyal American, regardless of his citizenship status.

The Supreme Court did not buy Ozawa's arguments. Only Caucasians were white, the court argued. They said that no matter what Ozawa did, he was of the Mongolian, not the Caucasian race, so he would not be eligible for naturalization.

Just a few months after Ozawa's case, the Supreme Court heard another petition for naturalization, this time by a man named Bhagat Singh Thind. Thind was an immigrant from India who had served in the U.S. army. Like Ozawa, Thind argued that he was white, but he presented his case differently than Ozawa. Indians, Thind said, were part of the Caucasian race, which made him white. He brought in biological experts to back up his argument.

While Thind used a different strategy than Ozawa, he ended up with the same result. The Supreme Court ruled that Thind wasn't white—even if he might have biologically been Caucasian, Indians simply weren't white. Thind could not become a U.S. citizen.

Citizenship for Native Americans

Native Americans were in North America long before the British settlers, the Constitution, or the 14th Amendment. Yet their citizenship was still questioned: in the 1884 case *Elk v. Wilkins*, the Supreme Court ruled that Native Americans were loyal to their tribes, and therefore did not fall under the jurisdiction of the U.S. government—meaning they were not born U.S. citizens, despite being born on U.S. soil.

Fact #16
★ ☆ ★

Native Americans were not granted birthright citizenship until the Indian Citizenship Act in 1924.

During World War I, a number of Native American soldiers fought on behalf of the United States, helping the country achieve victory. The Indian Citizenship Act of 1924 was passed in part to recognize the contributions of these soldiers, although it did not directly help them.

The Indian Citizenship Act stated that Native Americans born after its passage would automatically be citizens. However, it didn't retroactively grant citizenship to Native Americans who were already alive. Native Americans born before its passage were not granted citizenship until the passage of the Nationality Act of 1940.

Anyone can become a citizen

The United States continued to grapple with questions of immigration and citizenship throughout the 20th century. In 1952, Pat McCarran, a senator, and Francis Walter, a member of the House of Representatives, proposed the Immigration and Nationality Act of 1952, also known as the McCarran-Walter Act.

The McCarran-Walter Act was mostly designed to limit immigration. It established a preference system for immigrants, based on factors like work skills and family relations with U.S. citizens. It permanently banned certain people from immigrating to the United States—it especially targeted Communists, as the United States was in the midst of the Cold War with the Soviet Union. But while the McCarran-Walter Act imposed these restrictions, it also got rid of the specific racial restrictions in relation to U.S. citizenship.

Fact #17

★ ☆ ★

The Immigration and Nationality Act of 1952 declared that citizenship "shall not be denied or abridged because of race or sex," which allowed for anyone to become a U.S. citizen—regardless of their race, nationality, or gender—if they met the naturalization requirements.

President Harry Truman actually vetoed the Immigration and Nationality Act of 1952. He argued that its restrictions were discriminatory and un-American, but the House and the Senate overrode his veto, so the bill became a law. (If you need a review of how the U.S. legislative process works, that will be in Chapter 8).

Although immigration laws have continued to change since the 1950s, some elements of the Immigration and Nationality Act of 1952 are part of the naturalization process today. For example, individuals applying for naturalization are still asked whether they are, or ever have been, a member of the Communist Party, even though communists are no longer considered a major threat to the United States. Although the meaning of U.S. citizenship has changed over the course of the nation's history, this inquiry is a perfect example of how the legacy of American history remains in the citizenship process today.

CHAPTER 3

Obtaining Permanent Residency

P ermanent residency, which was discussed briefly in Chapter 1, is a necessary prerequisite for U.S. citizenship. How does someone become a U.S. permanent resident? Permanent residents are individuals who immigrated to the United States lawfully and have a green card allowing them to live and work.

Fact #18

★ ☆ ★

To become a U.S. citizen, a person must first obtain a visa and become a permanent resident.

People choose to immigrate for many reasons—to move closer to family, get a job, or escape persecution or violence. But lawfully immigrating to the United States isn't easy. Obtaining a visa requires filling out a lot of paperwork and typically costs money.

There are many different visas that grant a person the right to enter the United States. The type of visa that a person chooses depends on their reason for entry. Someone who is applying for a job has to fill out a different form than someone who wants to be united with their family. Some visa categories are limited—the federal government only gives out a certain number each year. This chapter will address the many kind of visas that individuals can use to enter the United States and how they can provide a pathway to permanent residency.

Fact #19

★ ☆ ★

An individual who has served honorably in the U.S. military during a time of war may become a citizen even without having ever been a U.S. permanent resident.

There is also one small exception to the permanent residency rule for U.S. citizenship. Special consideration is sometimes given to individuals who performed honorable service to the U.S. during a time of war. An individual who fought on behalf of the United States since September 11, 2001 might not need to be a permanent resident to acquire U.S. citizenship.

FAMILY VISAS

Any U.S. citizen can sponsor a visa for their immediate relatives. Immediate relatives refer to someone's spouse, parents, and children under age 21. The U.S. citizen who is sponsoring must be willing and able to accept both legal and financial responsibility for their relatives. A U.S. citizen hoping to sponsor their parents must be at least 21 years old. A stepparent can sponsor their stepchild if the parents' marriage took place before the stepchild turned 18.

Fact #20

★ ☆ ★

There are no limits on the number of family visas issued, and the visa process begins as soon as an application is submitted.

To petition for a relative, a U.S. citizen must fill out a Form I-130. Once that form is approved, the relative (who is living in another country) must fill out a Form I-485. Unlike many visa categories, the government does not restrict the number of visas issued to immediate relatives each year. As a result, individuals who are sponsored by an immediate family member have to wait a relatively short time—often less than a year.

Preference categories

Of course, spouses, parents, and children aren't the only relatives that U.S. citizens might want to sponsor visas for. Citizens can apply to sponsor visas for other family members. These relatives fall into four preference categories.

Fact #21

Family members who are not immediate relatives still have preference when applying for visas. However, there is a wait time for these preference visas.

The first preference category is for unmarried, adult sons and daughters of U.S. citizens. (For immigration law purposes, "adult" means over the age of 21). The second preference category is for spouses and unmarried children of U.S. permanent residents. The third preference category is for married son and daughters of U.S. citizens as well as their spouses and children, and the fourth preference category goes to brothers and sisters of U.S. citizens and their spouses and children.

As the phrase "preference categories" implies, some individuals are given priority over others based on their relation to the U.S. citizen who is sponsoring them. Additionally, the government only gives out a certain number of these family preference visas each year: 23,400 to people in the first preference category, 114,200 to people in the second preference category, 23,400 to people in the third preference category, and 65,000 to people in the fourth preference category. As a result of these limitations, individuals applying for a visa through the family preference categories may have to wait years before they can legally immigrate to the United States. Once they do immigrate, they become U.S. permanent residents.

Adoption

International adoption is another issue that brings together immigration and family. Parents from the United States who adopt a child from a foreign country understandably want their child to be a U.S. citizen. Luckily, there is a relatively straightforward citizenship process for adopted children.

Fact #22

★ ☆ ★

Both U.S. citizens and permanent residents can apply to adopt a child living in a foreign country. If either adoptive parent is a U.S. citizen, an adopted child becomes a U.S. citizen once the adoption is finalized.

Children adopted abroad by U.S. parents must first obtain a visa to enter the United States. There are several different ways to fill obtain this visa, depending on the specific details of the adoption. Children can enter the country along with their adoptive parents on this visa. If either parent is a U.S. citizen, an adopted child automatically becomes a U.S. citizen after two years in the United States.

Marriage

Marriage is another pathway to U.S. permanent residency. If two people are already married and one is a U.S. citizen, the partner who is not a citizen can apply for a green card via the family process described earlier in this chapter. Assuming the application is approved, that partner gains U.S. permanent residency status.

The inclusion of spouses in family visas makes sense — after all, families should be allowed to live together. However, it also creates a slight loophole: two individuals, one of whom is not from the United States, could get married just for the sake of getting a green card. Afterwards, they could get a divorce, but the formerly-from-a-foreign-country partner would still be a U.S. permanent resident.

Fact #23

★ ☆ ★

U.S. citizens sponsoring a visa for their spouse will have to provide evidence that the marriage is in good faith—that the couple genuinely loves each other and plans on creating a life together.

So-called "green-card marriages" are rare, although they've been portrayed in movies like Green Card (1991) and The Proposal (2009). Still, to ensure that individuals are married for reasons other than obtaining a visa, USCIS conducts interviews with couples applying for a marriage-based green card. A USCIS officer will separate the couple, and ask each partner questions about subjects like where they live, how they met, and how they do their finances. Then, the officer will compare each partner's answers to ensure they match up.

Immigration laws also allow for couples who are planning to marry — but haven't gotten married yet — to obtain a visa. These fiancé visas are not green cards, but allow the non-U.S. citizen partner to apply for permanent residency after the couple gets married.

CASE STUDY

"The process was fast and painless. I believe it was simplified because I am married to a member of the U.S. Armed Forces. I chose to naturalize so it may simplify any legal, succession, procedures. I have been for 15 years, my U.S. born husband and I own a house, and it made sense to transition."

— Nathalie

Fact #24

★ ☆ ★

U.S. citizens can petition for a fiancé visa for a fiancé from a foreign country. The couple must marry within 90 days, after which the fiancé visa expires. After marriage, the partner who is not a U.S. citizen can apply for permanent residency.

VAWA and permanent residency

The visa categories described in this section are dependent on sponsorship by a U.S. citizen. For the most part, this sponsorship is harmless, even helpful. However, there sadly are situations in which sponsoring citizens are abusive toward their relatives.

Fact #25
★ ☆ ★

The Violence Against Women Act (VAWA), passed in 1994, provides a pathway for women and children who are sponsored for a visa by a U.S. citizen or permanent resident to apply for permanent residency themselves if the person sponsoring their visa is abusive.

When sponsoring citizens are abusive, their relatives could be forced to stay with the abuser in order to main their U.S. permanent residency. VAWA allows individuals who are abused to petition for permanent residency themselves, without their abuser knowing, and therefore find safety and independence in the United States.

NON-FAMILY VISA OPTIONS

The first part of this chapter examined visa options based on family connections. But not everyone who wants to immigrate to the United States has a relative who a U.S. citizen! Luckily, there are other pathways to getting a visa and becoming a U.S. permanent resident. This next section will examine some of the other methods of visa acquisition.

Employment

The narrative of immigrants taking American jobs is a common part of United States history, from the days of Chinese laborers in California (as described in Chapter 2) to immigrants today. However, getting an American job as an immigrant isn't actually so simple.

Fact #26

★ ☆ ★

Before offering a job to an immigrant, an employer in the U.S. will have to advertise the job's availability and demonstrate that no qualified U.S. citizens or permanent residents have applied for it.

If a U.S.-based employer wants to offer a job to a foreign worker, they must also sponsor a visa for that worker. There are several kinds of job visas. Some of them are permanent worker visas, which allow a person to work in the United States and grant permanent residency. Others are temporary or contingent visas—they allow people to be in the country for a limited time, and only so long as they keep their job.

Permanent worker visas

As with family members, there are priority categories for individuals seeking to work in the United States. First preference, the highest priority workers, goes only to individuals with exceptional abilities. Despite the name, these visas aren't for any smart, talented people. They go to people who are famous within their field. For example, a foreign-born athlete might be admitted to the United States under one of these visas to play in an American sports league, or a famous actress might receive one to do a film in Hollywood. The USCIS website suggests that individuals provide a Pulitzer, and Oscar, or an Olympic medal as evidence that they deserve a first preference category visa. Individuals of extraordinary abilities can petition for a visa themselves, or have an employer petition for them. Either way, they will need a completed Form I-140.

The second preference category for employee visas goes to individuals who have substantial education and work experience. People seeking visas from this category must be applying for a job that requires an advanced degree—

such as a Master's degree or a Ph.D. Individuals don't apply for second preference category visas themselves. Instead, they apply for a job in the United States. If they are selected, the employer will fill out a Form I-140 on their behalf.

The third preference category for employee visas is for skilled workers and professionals. While these workers don't have to have the same knowledge or experience as second category employees, they must have work in a job that requires some training and is not seasonal. As with second category employees, their employers will fill out a Form I-140 to get them their visa.

The fourth preference category is a bit different from the previous three. Individuals who fit in this fourth category are known as special immigrants — they are people who hold, or have held in the past, particular jobs that give them special permission to enter the United States. Jobs that place a person in this fourth category include: religious workers, broadcasters, international employees who have worked for the U.S. government in a foreign country, Panama Canal Zone employees, and Afghan and Iraqi translators. Individuals can apply through this preference category using a Form I-360.

Fact #27

Employees in each of the four visa categories described so far are known as permanent workers once they are admitted to the United States, and can become permanent residents.

The fifth job-based preference category for immigrants is specifically for entrepreneurs — people hoping to start a business in the United States. To qualify for a visa from this fifth preference category, an individual must have at least $500,000 to invest in the United States and must hire at least 10 workers. To apply for a visa, a person must fill out a Form I-526.

People admitted to the United States as entrepreneurs are known as conditional permanent residents. They must prove to the government, typically within two years, that they have actually created jobs. Otherwise, they could lose their ability to live and work in the United States.

Once again, family also comes up in issues of immigration and employment. In order to keep families together, people who apply for visas in any of the five preference categories can also bring along their spouse and any children under the age of 21. Approximately 140,000 total permanent worker visas are available across all five preference categories.

Temporary work visas

Individuals can also obtain permission to work temporarily in the United States. These workers are known as temporary, or nonimmigrant workers. Opportunities for temporary work visas are available in many fields, including agricultural workers—who may come for just a few months for harvest season, people who transferred positions within a company, and members of foreign news organizations. These individuals are not eligible for permanent residency as a result of their work, and therefore are not on a pathway to citizenship.

Student visas

Smart, talented people from around the world come to the United States on student visas to study at colleges and universities. Student visas, like temporary work visas, are nonimmigrant visas, which means that foreign students are not permanent residents, nor are they on a pathway to citizenship. Many foreign students want to stay in the United States and keep working after they finish school. To do so, they can try to find a job that will sponsor permanent worker visa for them.

The green card lottery

Each year, the United States conducts a green card lottery, formally known as the Diversity Visa Lottery Program. The program hands out 50,000 green cards each year. They are given away lottery-style. Winners can apply for permanent residency, and have the chance to bring along their spouses and children.

Fact #28
★ ☆ ★

The green card lottery exists only for residents of countries with low rates of immigration to the United States.

However, the green card lottery isn't for everyone. In fact, the lottery is specifically designed for countries that do not send a lot of immigrants to the United States. Citizens of any country that has sent more than 50,000 immigrants to the United States in the past five years are not eligible to enter the green card lottery. Currently, these ineligible countries include: Bangladesh, Brazil, Canada, China, the Dominican Republic, El Salvador, Haiti, India, Mexico, Nigeria, Pakistan, Peru, Philippines, South Korea, the United Kingdom, and Vietnam.

CASE STUDY

"I am originally from Ireland. I obtained my citizenship by naturalization. I 'won' my Green Card (a Donnelly Visa) in 1993 in a lottery in which applicants were only allowed to send in one request. I then went through the whole process of getting U.S. citizenship. All I can remember after the ceremony is waiting in line to shake the hands of the judge to get my certificate of naturalization. What a great country!"   — Mick

Humanitarian visas

Many individuals want to immigrate—perhaps to join family or get a better job, as discussed earlier in this chapter. However, some people have no choice but to leave their homes. They may be caught up in the midst of a war, be persecuted because of their religion, race, sexuality, political beliefs, or have other reasons to fear for their lives.

Humanitarian visas are available for people who are fleeing such violence and persecution. These individuals are often known as refugees or asylum-seekers. Both U.S. and international law guide how refugees and asylum-seekers can seek permanent residency in the United States.

Fact #29

★ ☆ ★

Refugee status is a form of legal protection that can be granted to people who have been driven from their home and have a "well-founded fear of persecution on account of race, religion, nationality, membership in a particular social group, or political opinion," according to section 101(a)(42) of the Immigration and Nationality Act.

The terms refugee and asylum-seeker are often used interchangeably, but they have slightly distinct meanings. These sorts of distinctions are important when it comes to immigration law! A refugee refers to any person who has left their home due to violence or persecution. After leaving their home country, a refugee may choose to seek asylum in a specific country, making them an asylum-seeker in that country only.

Who decides where refugees go?
Refugees flee violence in many parts of the world. Most refugees don't come to United States. Instead, they move to neighboring countries, or go to a place where they have family. However, some refugees apply for resettlement—a process through the United Nations where they undergo interviews and background checks before eventually being granted asylum and resettled in a country where they are safe.

The United States has typically been one destination for United Nations resettlement, with Canada, Australia, and several Scandinavian countries also taking in refugees in recent years. The resettlement process is thorough, and often takes two years.

Applying for asylum

In addition to refugee resettlement through the United Nations process, the United States also grants asylum to certain individuals on a case-by-case basis. A person may apply for asylum if they are already residing in the United States, regardless of their immigration status. This means that undocumented immigrants can apply for asylum, as can people on temporary visas.

Fact #30

Asylum status can be granted to individuals who meet the requirements of a refugee and are already residing in the U.S.

People who apply for asylum in the United States first fill out a Form I-589. Unlike most immigration-related forms, there is no fee associated with Form I-589. Individuals must fill out this form within one year of arriving in the country, and ultimately have to go to court and make their case. They must explain why they have "credible fear" that they would be persecuted in their home country. They may call in experts or witnesses to help their case—other people who can testify about the struggles they face. A judge then rules on whether they deserve asylum status. An individual who is granted asylum becomes a U.S. permanent resident.

Temporary humanitarian visas

In additional to refugee and asylum claims, the United States also grants several categories of temporary humanitarian visas. As the name indicates, these visas only allow individuals to stay in the country for a limited amount of time. They do not grant people permanent residency or provide a pathway to U.S. citizenship.

Fact #31

★ ☆ ★

An individual can be granted Temporary Protected
Status (TPS) for between six and 18 months. An individual
might be granted TPS due to a temporarily conflict or
natural disaster that makes their home country
dangerous or inhospitable.

People living in the United States under TPS can apply for employment authorization—papers that give them the right to legally work as long as they are in the United States. However, these individuals are still expected to return to their home countries at some point.

Unlike with asylum status, where individuals must make their personal case for why they cannot return to their home country, the U.S. government chooses to grant TPS to citizens of an entire country, based on its assessment of that country's conditions. In the past, the U.S. government has granted TPS due to military conflicts and natural disasters. For example, Haitian citizens were granted TPS in the United States following a disastrous 7.0 magnitude earthquake in 2010.

Fact #32

★ ☆ ★

An individual who is not otherwise eligible for a
visa may be granted humanitarian parole, which would
allow them to temporarily visit the United States.
Like TPS, humanitarian parole does not help with
permanent residency.

Humanitarian parole is another form of temporary visa. Unlike TPS, it is granted to individuals on a case-by-case basis. Humanitarian parole might be given to some who is not allowed to enter the United States, perhaps because of a prior deportation, but who has good reason to—for example, to take care of a sick relative.

PEOPLE WITHOUT VISAS

So far, this chapter has discussed the legal options for people from other countries who want to come to the United States. However, not everyone immigrates legally. Approximately 11 million U.S. residents are known as undocumented immigrants or illegal aliens. They are people who do not have legal authorization to be in the United States, but still reside within its borders. Some undocumented immigrants snuck in across the border; many others used fake documents to get in. A number of undocumented people actually came to the country legally—for example, on a tourist visa—and stayed permanently.

Pathways to legalization for undocumented immigrants

Because undocumented immigrants broke the law to enter the country, they have few pathways to acquire permanent residency or citizenship. To acquire a green card, most undocumented immigrants would have to return to their home country and wait for three or ten years before applying for a visa.

Undocumented immigrants can gain legal status without leaving the United States a few different ways. The most common approach is through marriage to a U.S. citizen or legal permanent resident. Individuals can first apply for a provisional waiver, which would remove the requirement that they return to their home country, and then get sponsorship from their spouse.

Undocumented immigrants can also gain legal status in the United States if they have been, or could be, a victim of a serious crime. First, undocumented immigrants can apply for asylum, as discussed earlier in this chapter. Undocumented immigrants are also eligible for a U visa—a special visa created as part of a program to encourage people to comply with law enforcement. Because undocumented people in the United States are often at risk for deportation, many are reluctant to contact the police, even if they have been the victim of a serious crime. The U visa is for individuals who have been the victim of a serious crime and have information that will help law enforcement prosecute that crime. The U visa provides legal status, work authorization, and a pathway to permanent residence.

Get a lawyer!

Immigration rules are very complicated — this chapter only provides a basic summary of some of the visa types. In addition to the visas described in this chapter, there are other types of visas which are used less regularly. To complicate matters further, government policies about visas can change at any time. New laws and regulations affect the number of visas issued, who they are issued to, and other requirements.

The best advice for people who are uncertain about visas or immigration issues is to find an immigration lawyer. Lawyers are experts on the details of immigration law and the distinctions between different kinds of visas.

Immigration lawyers also tend to be very expensive. Individuals who cannot afford a lawyer should look to organizations that offer free or reduced-cost services. The American Immigration Lawyers Association helps some clients pro bono, and sites such **https://www.probono.net/** also provide useful information.

CASE STUDY

"Many people think that the path to citizenship is an easy one. The American Immigration Law Foundation (AILF) discovered that there is a misperception by the US public that all one needs to do to obtain citizenship is walk down to the local post office. To the contrary, the road to citizenship is a long one. At a minimum, an applicant cannot apply for citizenship unless they have been in permanent resident status for three years (if married to a US citizen) and five years for all other applicants.

Before becoming a citizen, a foreign national must become a permanent resident — another lengthy process that is designed primarily to the highly skilled labor force and immediate relative family members. Citizenship is not merely walking down to the post office, but rather it is a privilege that takes years to obtain."   — Kaushik

Kaushik is an immigration attorney practicing in San Francisco, California. He has helped hundreds of clients obtain visas and citizenship applications. Kaushik is also a member of the American Immigration Law Foundation, a prominent immigration non-profit organization dedicated to advancing fundamental fairness and due process under the law for immigrants.

CHAPTER 4

Requirements for Naturalization

The previous chapter addressed the ways individuals can immigrate to the United States and become permanent residents. Being a U.S. permanent resident has many benefits—for example, the ability to live and work anywhere in the United States—but permanent residents still miss out on several key aspects of U.S. citizenship, including the right to vote.

Fact #33
★ ☆ ★

To become a citizen, an individual must have already been lawfully admitted for permanent residence. That means people residing in the United States undocumented or on a temporary visa cannot apply for citizenship.

Permanent residents, however, have the opportunity to apply for citizenship through a process known as naturalization. Through the naturalization process, immigrants must earn their U.S. citizenship by taking tests about English and the American government and proving that they are people of good character.

WHO CAN BECOME A CITIZEN?

Not all permanent residents are eligible for U.S. citizenship. Before starting the naturalization process, individuals must make sure they meet several requirements.

Fact #34

★ ☆ ★

To become a citizen, an individual must be at least 18 years of age, have been a legal permanent resident for at least five years (or three years if married to a U.S. citizen), be of good moral character, be loyal to the United States, and be willing to take the Oath of Allegiance.

People under 18 cannot apply to be U.S. citizens; however, they do automatically become U.S. citizens if their parents are naturalized. Permanent residents must have lived in the country for five years—unless they are married to a U.S. citizen, in which case that requirement is only three years.

Fact #35

★ ☆ ★

During the previous five years, an applicant must not have been outside of the United States for a total period of more than 12 months.

Permanent residents are allowed to travel outside of the United States, but if they are gone too long, they lose their ability to apply for citizenship. If a person's vacations, travel for work, or other time spent outside the country total to more than 12 months in the past five years, than that individual will have to wait to apply for citizenship.

Fact #36
★ ☆ ★

Applicants who have served in the U.S. military may be exempt from the residency requirement.

There is one exception for individuals who have traveled outside the country—and that is members of the U.S. military. Many men and women who serve in the military spend much of their time overseas, as the United States has military bases all over the world. Denying people citizenship because they have been serving in the military seems to contradict American values, so people who have been serving the country overseas are still eligible to apply for U.S. citizenship, even though they haven't been in the country.

"Of good moral character"

While it is easy enough to measure the time a person has spent in the United States, some of the other requirements for citizenship are less objective. For example, to become U.S. citizens, people must be "of good moral character." How do you measure moral character? For the purposes of citizenship law, the United States ensures its new citizens are of good moral character by barring certain groups from becoming citizens.

Fact #37

People who have committed certain crimes may be barred from becoming U.S. citizens.

Murder—as well as other aggravated felonies, such as sexual assault or drug trafficking—can make an individual permanently barred from becoming a U.S. citizen. Certain lower-level crimes, such as fraud or illegal gambling, make individuals temporarily ineligible for citizenship. Typically, a person must wait five years after committing one of these crimes before becoming eligible for U.S. citizenship.

Fact #38

Individuals who were every part of the Nazi party, the Communist party, or other totalitarian parties or terrorist organizations may be permanently barred from becoming U.S. citizens.

To judge for moral character, the United States also prohibits people from certain extreme political parties or groups from obtaining citizenship. These political limitations tell a bit about American history. For example, communists were barred from U.S. citizenship by the Immigration and Naturalization Act of 1952 (from Chapter 2). When that law was passed, the United States was in the middle of the Cold War, and communists seemed like a real threat. Today, the government is less worried about communism, but that portion of the law remains.

Knowing America

Becoming an American citizen brings many rights and responsibilities. People who want to become citizens must be aware of what they will be expected to do. To ensure new citizens are prepared, there are several requirements about what people seeking naturalization must know.

Fact #39
★ ☆ ★

To become a naturalized citizen, an individual must be able to read, write, and understand English and have a basic knowledge of American history, the U.S. government, and the Constitution.

Although the United States does not have an official language, English is by far the most commonly used language in the country. People applying for citizenship don't have to speak English perfectly, but they must understand it well enough to carry out their responsibilities as a citizen.

The responsibilities of citizenship—such as the right to vote—require people to understand how the U.S. government works. Therefore, people who want to be naturalized citizens must show that they understand the basics of American history and civics.

Fact #40
★ ☆ ★

People who are elderly or have a disability may be exempt from the English and civics requirements for naturalization.

As with many parts of citizenship law, there is a small exception to the language and civics requirements for naturalization. Some people may want to become U.S. citizens, but because of their age or disability, they may be unable to pass an English or history test. Therefore, the law provides an exception in certain cases to allow elderly or disabled people to become citizens, even if they don't meet a few of the standards.

THE APPLICATION PROCESS

There are many people in the United States who speak English, understand American history and government, are of good moral character, and are loyal to the country. But being all these things doesn't magically give a person citizenship — people still must go through a long, rigorous process to prove to the U.S. government that they meet these requirements.

The N-400 form

Fact #41
★ ☆ ★

The application for naturalization — the form anyone must fill out to begin the process of becoming a U.S. citizen — is known as the N-400 form.

The naturalization process begins with paperwork. The N-400 form — the first piece of paper for people applying for citizenship — has 18 sections. It must be filled out in black ink. The form asks basic questions, such a person's name, age, and address. It also asks about their past — where were they born? What country are they a citizen of? It asks about marriage, family, and job history.

The N-400 form also asks a number of questions to answer the "good moral character" issue addressed in the previous section. For example, one question reads: "Did you EVER recruit (ask), enlist (sign up), conscript (require), or use any person under 15 years of age to serve in or help an armed force or group?" Individuals who helped recruit child soldiers would likely be deemed to have poor moral character, and might be denied citizenship.

Background checks

Fact #42
★ ☆ ★

In addition to the N-400 form, an individual applying for citizenship must submit two passport-style photographs and a copy of their permanent resident card, and pay two fees: a $640 naturalization fee and an $85 biometric fee—to cover the cost of fingerprinting.

While a person applying for citizenship tells their own story on their N-400 form, the government also wants to verify that their information is accurate. To cover the cost of verifying claims and completing the citizenship process, people must pay several fees when they turn in their N-400 form.

Fact #43
★ ☆ ★

After an individual submits an N-400 form, they will have to complete a biometrics appointment. USCIS will take their photo and fingerprints so the FBI can run a background check.

A background check is another way the government verifies that an individual is of good moral character. If a person has been convicted of a crime in the United States, it will likely come up — and depending on the severity, that individual may be denied citizenship.

The interview

Assuming a person's N-400 form is accepted and nothing strange comes up during a background check, USCIS will set up an interview. The interview consists of two main parts: the citizenship test (which will be discussed in more detail in Chapter 9) and the question-and-answer with a USCIS officer.

Fact #44
★ ☆ ★

An individual applying for naturalization will have a naturalization interview. At this interview, they will answer questions from a USCIS officer and take their English and civics tests.

Citizenship interviews take place at USCIS offices in cities throughout the United States. Applicants must bring their permanent residence card to the interview — it serves as a form of identification. The interview is under oath, meaning applicants must swear to tell the truth during the entire process. A person who is found to lie during their interview will likely be denied U.S. citizenship.

During the question-and-answer part of the interview, the USCIS officer asks the person seeking citizenship about their application. Subjects of conversation may include the person's background, their country of origin, and their loyalty to the United States. The officer will ask about information on the N-400 form, as well as anything that came up when the government conducted a background check.

The Oath of Allegiance

USCIS gives applicants the results of their citizenship test immediately after the interview. There are three possible results: the application for citizenship can be granted, continued, or denied. If an application is granted, the individual will almost be a citizen—there's just one more step!

Fact #45

★ ☆ ★

If an individual's application for citizenship is approved, they will be scheduled to take the Oath of Allegiance at a naturalization ceremony. A person does not become a citizen until they take the Oath of Allegiance!

The Oath of Allegiance is the final step in the citizenship process. While new citizens have been required to take an oath since the first Immigration and Nationality Act in 1790, there was no standardized Oath of Allegiance until 1929. The oath has undergone a few modifications since then. It currently goes as follows:

> *I hereby declare, on oath, that I absolutely and entirely renounce and abjure all allegiance and fidelity to any foreign prince, potentate, state, or sovereignty, of whom or which I have heretofore been a subject or citizen; that I will support and defend the Constitution and laws of the United States of America against all enemies, foreign and domestic; that I will bear true faith and allegiance to the same; that I will bear arms on behalf of the United States when required by the law; that I will perform noncombatant service in the Armed Forces of the United States when required by the law; that I will perform work of national importance under civilian direction when required by the law; and that I take this obligation freely, without any mental reservation or purpose of evasion; so help me God.*

Fact #46

A judge or USCIS officer administers the Oath of Allegiance at a naturalization ceremony. Many people of different national origins typically become citizens at a naturalization ceremony together.

Sometimes, people can complete their citizenship test and take the Oath of Allegiance in the same day; other times, they may have to wait several months. Many naturalization ceremonies happen in courtrooms; others take place in schools or other public venues; sometimes special naturalization ceremonies are held at notable historical landmarks.

If something goes wrong . . .

Most of the time, USCIS approves individuals' citizenship applications, but occasionally, issues come up. Rather than granting citizenship, USCIS can choose to continue someone's application—put the application on hold and seek more information. There are two situations where USCIS might continue an application. First, a person will receive this designation if they fail the English or citizenship tests. In this case, the individual will have one more chance to take the tests, usually with two or three months. If they fail again, their application will be denied.

USCIS may also deny an application if someone is deemed ineligible for naturalization for any of the reasons discussed earlier in this chapter. If an individual's application for citizenship is denied, they will receive a written notice from USCIS explaining why.

Most of the time, however, citizenship applications are approved. According to USCIS, the naturalization process typically takes six months from start to finish. After this six month period—and the related paperwork, tests, and interview—an individual becomes a U.S. citizen for the rest of their life.

CHAPTER 5

Benefits and Costs of Naturalization

The previous chapter addressed naturalization—how individuals can legally become U.S. citizens. The process is long and winding, so most people do not take the decision to become a U.S. citizen lightly. Instead, they must think about what they gain, and lose, when they choose to apply for citizenship.

This chapter will address the benefits and costs of naturalization. It will talk about the special privileges that only U.S. citizens can access, and discuss what immigrants may lose if they apply for U.S. citizenship.

BENEFITS OF U.S. CITIZENSHIP

Some of the benefits of U.S. citizenship have already been discussed in this book. Only citizens can vote, and therefore participate in one of the most essential parts of democracy. Living in the United States as a citizen is easier than as a permanent resident. As discussed in Chapter 2, permanent residents must renew their visas, which is expensive and requires a lot of paperwork.

Family benefits

Chapter 3 outlined the many ways family provides an advantage when it comes to immigration and visas. Family also has a special role in the naturalization process—both for the people who become U.S. citizens, and their relatives.

Fact #47

★ ☆ ★

When adults naturalize, their children who are under the age of 18 and are lawful permanent residents also become citizens.

Only people over the age of 18 can fill out naturalization paperwork, but children under that age can still become naturalized citizens. In fact, the citizenship process is incredibly simple: children under the age of 18 automatically become U.S. citizens if they are living in the United States and one of their parents chooses to naturalize. These children can obtain proof of citizen by filling out an N-600 form.

Some individuals who naturalize are lucky to already have their family in the United States. However, many others have relatives—such as parents, children, or a spouse—who are still living in another country.

Fact #48

★ ☆ ★

Naturalized citizens can sponsor family visas for their family members living in foreign countries.

U.S. citizens can sponsor their relatives on family visas, allowing them to come to the United States and become permanent residents. This is particularly relevant for naturalized citizens—many were once immigrants and still have family members in other countries.

For example, a foreign student may come to the United States from China on a student visa to attend college and eventually get a job that gives her permanent residency. If, after five years as a permanent resident, she decides to become a citizen, she would be able to sponsor her parents to join her.

Jobs and aid

In addition to the opportunity to reunite with family members, citizenship also opens up a new set of possibilities for individuals in the United States. In particular, citizens have access to government jobs and benefits.

Fact #49

★ ☆ ★

Many government jobs require U.S. citizenship.

Executive Order 11935—signed by President Gerald Ford in 1976— dictates that only U.S. citizens can be hired for jobs with the federal government. Although there are a few exceptions to this law, U.S. citizens certainly have a better chance at getting hired than non-citizens.

Fact #50

★ ☆ ★

Citizens have an easier time getting government benefits.

Government benefits, such as food stamps and Medicaid, are available to some types of immigrants. However, applying for benefits can be easier for U.S. citizens, and generally requires less paperwork.

U.S. passport

A passport is a form of identification that individuals use to travel between countries. Every country in the world issues passports to its own citizens, and people who immigrate to the United States first entered the country with a passport from their home country.

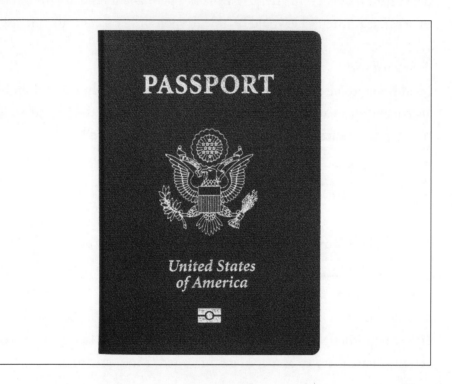

Fact #51
★ ☆ ★

Any U.S. citizen can obtain a U.S. passport, which is needed to travel outside of the country. Adults typically must renew their passport every 10 years.

Once someone becomes a U.S. citizen, they can apply for a U.S. passport, which they can use to travel to other countries. To get a passport, individuals must fill out a form and get their picture taken. Passport applications can be submitted at local Post Offices.

Fact #52

★ ☆ ★

With a U.S. passport, citizens can visit nearly any country in the world.

The U.S. passport allows people to travel to nearly any country in the world! Over 100 countries allow visa-free travel for U.S. citizens, which means people can visit these countries on vacation without having to complete any additional paperwork. Only a few countries, such as Iran and North Korea, make it difficult for U.S. citizens to visit.

Freedom from deportation

As mentioned in Chapter 1, non-citizens in the United States can still be at risk for deportation. Even U.S. permanent residents who have been living in the country for decades can still be deported if they are convicted of a crime.

Fact #53

★ ☆ ★

U.S. citizens, even those who have been naturalized, never have to worry about being deported.

Deportation can be scary —people who have been living in the United States for a long time may not have connections in their home country, or might not even speak the language. Becoming a U.S. citizen assures that a person can never be deported.

COSTS OF NATURALIZATION

If there are so many benefits to becoming a U.S. citizen, why don't all permanent residents choose to naturalize? Although U.S. citizenship has many benefits, it also has several costs. People must weigh these benefits and costs, and decide for themselves whether naturalization is the right choice.

What is there to lose?

Permanent residents who feel deeply connected to the United States, who plan on spending the rest of their lives in the country, and who have a firm understanding of the naturalization process have little to lose by applying for citizenship. But not everyone follows this path. In particular, people may choose to not become U.S. citizens because of their loyalty to another country, for financial reasons, or because applying for naturalization might cause them other problems.

Dual citizens

The United States generally allows its citizens to have dual citizenship. As discussed in Chapter 1, dual citizens are people who are citizens of two countries at the same time.

Fact #54
★ ☆ ★

Some individuals must give up their citizenship in their home country to become a U.S. citizen.

However, not all countries allow dual citizenship. As a result, some people who apply for naturalization in the United States will have to forfeit their citizenship in their home country, and therefore give up certain rights. Not everyone wants to do this—and so some people choose to remain U.S. permanent residents, rather than applying for citizenship.

Financial costs

Applying for citizenship costs money. The naturalization fee is currently $640, and the biometrics fee (as discussed in Chapter 4) is $85. These fees do cost more than the fees associated with renewing a permanent residency visa. For some people, obtaining the $725 to apply for citizenship is too expensive—so they choose not to apply.

Fact #55

★ ☆ ★

USCIS grants fee waivers for certain individuals who cannot afford to apply for naturalization.

Many people do not realize that they can receive for a fee waiver if the cost of applying for citizenship is prohibitively high. To apply for a waiver, individuals must fill out an I-912 form, which asks about their income, their household, and any government benefits they receive. USCIS evaluates their answers to these questions and issues fee waivers on a case-by-case basis.

Taxes

People who live and work in the United States pay U.S. taxes, regardless of their immigration or citizenship status. However, U.S. citizens living abroad must still pay the U.S. government income taxes (taxes they earn on the money they get from their job) as well as other kinds of taxes.

Becoming a U.S. citizen might not make sense for someone who plans to live in the United States for a period of time and then move elsewhere. For some people, the long-term cost of still having to pay U.S. taxes while residing in another country might outweigh the short-term benefits of citizenship.

Obtaining legal advice

Earlier in this chapter, freedom from deportation was listed as one of the benefits of applying for naturalization. It is true that people who become U.S. citizens can never be deported. However, for some people, issues can arise during the naturalization process which could lead to deportation.

Fact #57
★ ☆ ★

When a person initiates the naturalization process,
USCIS examines their history. If the person has been
convicted of criminal acts, acquired their visa
illegally, or has committed a deportable offense since
receiving permanent residence status, their application
for naturalization will be denied and they could
be deported.

Although people who are convicted of certain crimes are eligible for deportation, not everyone who is eligible gets deported. Sometimes, courts fail to coordinate with Immigrations and Customs Enforcement. Other times, the court may decide to make an exception, and allow someone who is eligible for deportation to stay in the United States. However, if these individuals apply for citizenship, USCIS will examine their records and notice their history—and there is a chance they will be deported.

Some people may not be sure whether they are eligible to apply for citizenship, or whether their past actions might lead to their deportation. Immigration lawyers can help people understand the complexities of immigration and citizenship law, and determine the right course of action.

Fact #58
★ ☆ ★

Immigration lawyers can help individuals manage the paperwork and strategy necessary to obtain citizenship. However, lawyers often cost thousands of dollars.

Immigration lawyers are expensive, but—for individuals who are uncertain about the benefits and costs of applying for U.S. citizenship—they are often a good investment. Refer to the resources listed at the end of Chapter 3 to learn ways to find legal advice.

CHAPTER 6

American History

One of the requirements for naturalization is that people must have a good understanding of American history and the U.S. government. This chapter will address the major history topics that people seeking naturalization are required to know, while the next two chapters will talk about politics and government.

American history is a broad subject, covering hundreds of years across a large nation. New citizens are not responsible for knowing every fact and story, but they do have to have a general idea of how the country came to be. USCIS provides an overview of the major history topics on its website; this chapter will address those same subjects.

THE COLONIAL PERIOD AND INDEPENDENCE

The encounter that ultimately led to the founding of the United States took place in 1492, when an Italian sailor named Christopher Columbus—traveling on behalf of the Spanish—landed on an island in the Caribbean Sea. Columbus hadn't been trying to find a new continent. He had been hoping to sail to Asia, where he could trade for spices. However, his accidental landing would have serious consequences, for both the Europeans he represented and the people he encountered.

Columbus himself never visited the territory that is now the United States. However, his encounter led many other explorers from many other countries to sail across the Atlantic Ocean, searching for territory of their own.

The first European settlers

In the late 1500s and early 1600s, British ships set off to establish colonies in North America. The first permanent British colony was established in Jamestown, Virginia, in 1607. Settlers established another colony in Plymouth, Massachusetts, in 1620.

Fact #59
★ ☆ ★

Early settlers came to America in the 1600s and 1700s for a variety of reasons: to escape persecution, practice their religion freely, and find economic opportunity.

Moving to North America was not easy for these early settlers. They had to endure a long boat ride, only to land in a place they had never seen before, where they would have to largely fend for themselves. However, some people found this challenge worthwhile. Many of the early settlers were facing religious persecution in their home country. Moving to America allowed them to practice their religion freely.

Other early settlers were seeking economic opportunities. Many Europeans were very poor—but if they moved to America, they could start over with their own land and create a better life for their families.

Native Americans

Fact #60
★ ☆ ★

When the European colonizers arrived, Native Americans had already been living in North America for thousands of years.

Early settlers liked to think that America was full of land for them to take. But millions of Native Americans were already living on the continent. At times, the Native Americans were accommodating to the settlers. In Plymouth, for example, Native Americans initially helped the British settlers survive the harsh winter.

However, Native Americans did not always take kindly to the European intrusion on their land. At times, violence broke out between the settlers and Native Americans. The Native Americans were also weakened by diseases that the Europeans brought over.

The British colonies

Fact #61
★ ☆ ★

Although colonizers came from all over Europe, the majority of people who settled in what would become the United States were from Britain.

Since the majority of settlers in North America were British, the British government felt responsible for governing them. Between 1607 and 1732, the British government founded 13 formal colonies. While the colonies chose some of their own leaders, they still had to follow orders of the British king.

Fact #62

★ ☆ ★

Britain founded 13 colonies in North America: Delaware, Pennsylvania, New Jersey, Georgia, Connecticut, Massachusetts, Maryland, South Carolina, New Hampshire, Virginia, New York, North Carolina, and Rhode Island.

The British colonies were very different from each other. Some, like Rhode Island and Maryland, were founded as religious sanctuaries for people who were persecuted. Others were founded for economic reasons. In many of the Southern colonies, settlers discovered that they could grow a lot of tobacco. The tobacco industry grew rapidly, bringing in profits—and attracting more settlers.

Fact #63

★ ☆ ★

The colonizers brought people across the ocean from Africa to work as slaves. Slaves were not paid, nor were they given access to basic rights.

However, the British needed lots of workers to grow tobacco and other crops in the new colonies. They relied on bringing in slaves from Africa. Through the Atlantic Slave Trade, millions of Africans were taken from their homes and shipped across the ocean. Many of these slaves went to South America or the Caribbean, but nearly 400,000 were sent to the British colonies in North America.

Slaves in the British colonies often worked under brutal conditions. While the colonists had come to America seeking religious freedom and economic opportunities, slaves were denied their freedom and the right to make a life for themselves.

The war for independence

Although the people living in the 13 colonies were technically subjects of the British king, not all of them felt loyal to the British government. Between 1754 and 1763, the colonists fought alongside the British Empire as part of the French and Indian War (also known as the Seven Years' War, although it lasted nine years). The British and the colonists ultimately won the war against the French and the Native Americans, but afterwards, the British government increased taxes on the colonists to pay for the costs of the war.

The colonists were not happy about the British taxes. Tensions were particularly high in the city of Boston, Massachusetts. In 1770, British soldiers shot at angry colonists who were throwing snowballs. Five colonists were killed, and the event became known as the Boston Massacre. In 1773, colonists in Boston protested British taxes by sneaking onto British ships in the middle of the middle of the night and throwing tea into the harbor. In response, the British government passed a series of laws called the Coercive Acts, which were designed to punish the colonies.

In response to the Coercive Acts, many colonists in Massachusetts began to openly rebel. Some of them even began to build their own militias to fight against the British. In April 1775, the British army decided to seize some colonial munitions that were stored in the town of Concord, Massachusetts.

Fact #64

★ ☆ ★

The Revolutionary War began in 1775 with battles at
Lexington and Concord in Massachusetts.

The colonists heard about the British plan and decided to fight. The colonial army ended up battling the British army in Lexington, Massachusetts, as well as Concord. These two battles marked the beginning of the American Revolutionary War.

The Declaration of Independence

As the Revolutionary War continued, certain colonial leaders began to think that the colonies would be better off if they were entirely separate from Great Britain. In 1776, representatives from all 13 colonies met in Philadelphia, Pennsylvania. They called their meeting the Second Continental Congress. Historians often refer to the members of the Second Continental Congress as the Founding Fathers, because their actions led to the founding of the United States.

Fact #65

★ ☆ ★

Thomas Jefferson wrote the Declaration of Independence, which declared the 13 colonies to be their own country, separate from Great Britain. Representatives at the Second Continental Congress adopted the Declaration of Independence on July 4, 1776.

The Declaration of Independence listed many of the colonists' complaints against King George III, the British king, and said that these complaints gave colonists the right to rebel against the British and declare themselves independent.

Fact #66

★ ☆ ★

The Declaration of Independence stated that all individuals ought to have the right to life, liberty, and the pursuit of happiness.

The Declaration of Independence was unique because it argued that all people had legal and human rights: "We hold these truths to be self-evident, that all men are created equal, that they are endowed by their Creator with certain unalienable Rights, that among these are Life, Liberty and the pursuit of Happiness." Thus, the Declaration of Independence established equality and freedom as essential American principles, which would guide the nation for years to come.

Fact #67

★ ☆ ★

Independence Day is a national holiday celebrated on July 4 every year to commemorate the signing of the Declaration of Independence.

The rest of the war

The Revolutionary War continued after the signing of the Declaration of Independence. Although the British soldiers were trained and equipped better than the American rebel soldiers, the Americans fought valiantly. The American army was led by General George Washington and received aid from the French because France did not like Great Britain.

In 1781, British soldiers surrendered to the American army at the Battle of Yorktown, in Yorktown, Virginia. In 1783, British and American leaders formally signed the Treaty of Paris, which granted the colonies their independence.

After the war

Free from British rule, the former colonies—now known as the United States—were responsible for governing themselves. However, they immediately ran into some problems. In 1777, while the colonies were still at war, the Continental Congress had adopted the Articles of Confederation, an agreement between the colonies about basic laws and the structure of the government.

Fact #68

★ ☆ ★

The 13 original colonies became the first 13 states of the United States.

The Articles of Confederation did not provide a strong foundation for the new United States. The Articles gave most of the power to the individual states, and so there was almost know way to enforce laws equally across the states. Individual states came up with their own currencies (forms of money), which made it difficult for people from one state to do business with people from another. Furthermore, the federal government was not allowed to tax its citizens, so it could not raise money to pay of the debts from the Revolutionary War.

The Constitution

The Founding Fathers realized that the Articles of Confederation were failing. In 1787, they gathered once again in Philadelphia. Originally, their goal was to fix the problems with the Articles of Confederation. However, as they began working, they realized that they were better off throwing out the Articles entirely, and creating a whole new system of government.

Fact #69

★ ☆ ★

The Constitution was written by delegates from 12 of the 13 states (all except Rhode Island) at the Constitutional Convention during the summer of 1787.

The delegates who gathered in Philadelphia ultimately came up with the U.S. Constitution. The Constitution provided for a stronger national government than the Articles of Confederation. (The contents of the Constitution will be discussed more thoroughly in the next chapter). However, not everybody embraced the Constitution right away.

Fact #70
★ ☆ ★

James Madison, Alexander Hamilton, and John Jay wrote a series of essays known as The Federalist Papers with a goal of increasing popular support for the Constitution.

For the Constitution to go into effect, it had to be ratified by at least nine of the 13 colonies. On June 21, 1788, New Hampshire became the ninth state to ratify the Constitution, and the states agreed that the Constitution would formally take effect on March 4, 1789. George Washington, the hero of the Revolutionary War, was named the first president.

Fact #71
★ ☆ ★

George Washington became the first president of the United States in 1789. He is sometimes known as the "Father of Our Country."

THE 1800S

As the United States moved into the 1800s, the country continued to grow and expand. However, the century wasn't an easy one. The United States also got involved in several wars, and grappled with difficult issues, such as slavery and women's rights.

Fact #72

★ ☆ ★

In 1803, the United States purchased the Louisiana Territory from France. The purchase nearly doubled the size of the country!

The Louisiana Purchase, authorized by President Thomas Jefferson in 1803, granted the United States access to about 827,000 square miles of land west of the Mississippi River. The United States paid $15 million for the land, which helped France pay some of its own debts.

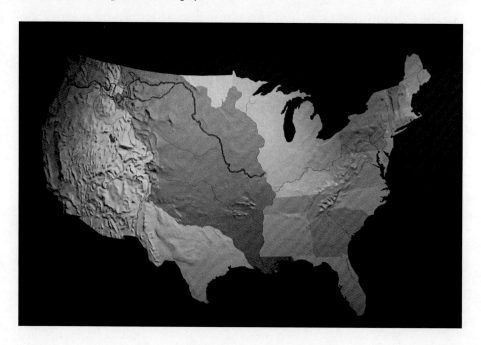

Early wars

Although the United States had a friendly relationship with France, its relationship with Great Britain was less stellar. Because Britain was at war with France, Britain tried to limit trade between the United States and

France. Furthermore, to ensure it had enough people in its Navy, the British began impressing American sailors who had been born in Britain — forcing them to join the British Navy, even if they considered themselves American.

While the United States was in conflict with Britain at sea, it also faced conflicts with Native Americans on land. As American settlers tried to expand westward in the Northwest Territories (the area made up of the modern-day states of Ohio, Illinois, Indiana, Michigan, and Wisconsin), they faced opposition from the Native Americans, who did not want the settlers to take their land. The British, who occupied the neighboring territory of Canada, generally supported the Native Americans against the American settlers.

The War of 1812

The tension finally boiled over in 1812, when the United States declared war on Britain. Although the two countries had been in conflict for a while, neither was particularly prepared for war. Britain was in conflict with Portugal and Spain at the time, while the U.S. army was disorganized and lacked central leadership.

Fact #73

The War of 1812 was fought between the United States and Britain. It lasted from 1812 until 1815.

During the war, American troops invaded Canada, but were ultimately beaten back by British troops. Meanwhile, the British Navy made a series of attacks in Chesapeake Bay area, including an attack on Washington D.C., the capital.

Fact #74

★ ☆ ★

In August 1814, the British burned down the White House, which was at the time the home of President James Madison.

At the end of 1814, Britain and France became closer allies, so Britain decided to allow the United States to trade with France once again and stopped impressing American sailors. As a result, the two countries no longer had much reason to fight. In December, they signed the Treaty of Ghent, formally ending the war.

However, communication wasn't very good in the 1800s; news of the Treaty of Ghent didn't reach the American and British armies right away, so they kept fighting. In January 1815, General Andrew Jackson won a significant victory at the Battle of New Orleans. Shortly thereafter, both sides realized the war was over, and the British Navy left.

The Mexican-American War

While the United States was once the property of Great Britain, Mexico had belonged to Spain until 1821. When Mexico first became a country, it was much larger than it is today, and included much of the territory that is now states like California, Arizona, Nevada, Utah, New Mexico, and Texas.

In 1836, Texas seceded from Mexico, becoming its own country. Many of the people living in Texas were American settlers, so the United States annexed Texas in 1845. However, the border between Texas and Mexico was not well-defined, and both the United States and Mexico claimed that they owned the land between the Nueces River and the Rio Grande. The United States offered to buy the land from Mexico, but Mexico refused. President James Polk ordered American troops to invade Mexico.

Fact #75

★ ☆ ★

The Mexican-American War was fought between the United States and Mexico from 1846 until 1848.

During the war, the United States took control of most of Mexico's northern territories. The United States also invaded central Mexico and captured the capital, Mexico City. As a result, Mexico surrendered in 1848.

Fact #76

★ ☆ ★

As a result of the Mexican-American war, the United States won a lot of territory from Mexico — once again expanding the size of the nation.

The two nations signed the Treaty of Guadalupe Hidalgo in 1848. The treaty granted most of Northern Mexico to the United States. This land would later become the states of California, Arizona, Nevada, Utah, and New Mexico.

The Civil War

Although the Declaration of Independence stated that "all men are created equal," not everyone in the United States had equal rights — African-Americans were still forced to work as slaves in some part of the country. While most of the Northern states had abolished slavery, most Southern states still relied on it, as slaves made cotton production very profitable.

During the 1800s, many new states became a part of the United States. Each time, these states were admitted as either slave states, meaning slavery was legal, or free states, where slavery was not allowed. Representatives from Southern states worried that, if too many free states joined the country, then they would have to power to outlaw slavery in the entire country.

Fact #77

★ ☆ ★

In the Civil War, the Northern states fought against the Southern ones. The Southern states seceded from the Union because they were worried the federal government would abolish slavery.

In 1860, Abraham Lincoln was elected president of the United States. While Lincoln did not favor immediately ending slavery, he believed that new states should not be allowed to have slavery. The Southern states did not like Lincoln, so they decided to fight rather than accept his presidency.

Fact #78

★ ☆ ★

Abraham Lincoln was president of the United States during the Civil War. He is often credited with saving the Union during a time of crisis.

The course of war

The Southern states founded their own country, which they called the Confederate States of America. Confederate soldiers fought against soldiers from the United States. Most of the battles were fought in the Southern states.

Fact #79

★ ☆ ★

In 1863, Lincoln issued the Emancipation Proclamation, declaring that all slaves in Southern states were free. After the war, the 13th Amendment formally declared the end of slavery in all of the United States.

The war lasted until 1865. On April 14, 1865, President Lincoln was shot by John Wilkes Booth, a Confederate sympathizer. Lincoln died the next morning. Andrew Johnson, Lincoln's vice president, became the president. The Southern states formally surrendered in May.

The Spanish-American War

In 1898, an American ship called the USS Maine blew up in a harbor in Havana, Cuba. At the time, Cuba still belonged to Spain. Although the explosion of the USS Maine was likely an accident, the United States blamed Spain and the two countries went to war.

Fact #80
★ ☆ ★

The Spanish-American War was fought between Spain and the United States in 1898. As a result of the war, the United States acquired the territories of Guam, Puerto Rico, and the Philippines.

The Spanish-American war lasted only 10 weeks, as the U.S. Navy proved to be much stronger than Spain. The two nations signed a treaty in Paris, in which the United States agreed to pay Spain $20 million in exchange for its overseas territories.

Social issues in the 1800s

The 1800s were also a time of significant social change. With the growth of cities, more women began working outside of the home, and many began to believe that women deserved equal rights as men.

Fact #81

★ ☆ ★

Susan B. Anthony fought for women's rights during the 1800s, including the right to vote. Although she died in 1906 — 14 years before American women gained voting rights — she is remembered as a leader in the suffrage movement.

Voting rights were an essential component of the women's rights movement. Women fighting for voting rights were known as suffragists. In 1869, the territory of Wyoming became the first place in the United States where women were allowed to vote. Women won voting rights nationally with the passage of the 19th Amendment in 1920.

THE EARLY 20TH CENTURY

During the early 1900s, both the United States and the world encountered several major crises. Although the country endured these hardships, many people suffered due to war and economic struggles.

World War I

In June 1914, Archduke Franz Ferdinand, the heir to the Austro-Hungarian throne, was shot by a Serbian nationalist in Bosnia. This incident may have seemed isolated, but a complicated system of political alliances soon brought most of Europe into a war.

Fact #82
★ ☆ ★

World War I began in Europe in 1914. The United States intervened on the side of the Allied Powers (led by Britain, France, and Italy) against the Central Powers (led by Germany, Austria-Hungary, and the Ottoman Empire).

American involvement

The United States did not want to take part in the European conflict. After all, America was separated from Europe by the vast Atlantic Ocean. In 1916, President Woodrow Wilson ran for reelection saying that he would keep the country out of war.

Fact #83
★ ☆ ★

Woodrow Wilson was President of the United States from 1913 until 1921. He initially tried to keep the United States out of World War I, but eventually decided that American involvement in the war was necessary.

However, the United States grew angry because German submarines kept attacking American passenger ships. In April 1917, Congress formally declared war against Germany. With the help of American troops, the Allied

Powers eventually won the war. The two sides declared an armistice on November 11, 1918, and formally signed a treaty the following year.

The Great Depression

The 1920s were a good time for many Americans. The economy flourished following World War I, and people thought the country would keep growing. It turned out they were very wrong.

Fact #84

★ ☆ ★

Following the stock market crash in October 1929, the United States entered a severe economic recession known as the Great Depression.

The stock market crash of 1929 was followed by one of the most severe economic downturns in history. Unemployment rose to 25 percent, and many Americans lost their jobs. Agricultural prices dropped substantially, and many farmers could not afford to keep growing their crops. To make matters worse, many Midwestern states were hit with severe weather, further damaging farms and destroying people's livelihoods.

The United States was not the only country affected by the Great Depression. Global trade declined substantially during the depression, making every country worse off. Many European countries, which were still facing debts from World War I, especially struggled.

Franklin D. Roosevelt

In 1932, Franklin D. Roosevelt was elected president of the United States. Roosevelt promised to restore the American economy. He enacted a policy known as the New Deal, which focused on three principles: relief for poor and unemployed people, economic recovery, and reform to ensure that such a crisis would never happen again.

Fact #85

★ ☆ ★

Franklin D. Roosevelt was elected president in 1932. He guided the country through both the Great Depression and World War II.

Roosevelt's policies were more effective than those of the previous president, Herbert Hoover. Unemployment slowly dropped during the 1930s, although the economy was still struggling compared to the 1920s. As it turned out, the economy would soon cease to be Roosevelt's biggest problem — instead, the United States once again found itself involved in a world war.

World War II

In 1933, Adolf Hitler seized power in Germany. Hitler, who felt Germany had been humiliated after its loss in World War I, wanted to restore German greatness. He blamed Jews for most of Germany's problems. After annexing Austria and Czechoslovakia, Germany invaded Poland in 1939. As a result, Britain and France—who were allies of Poland—declared war on Germany.

American involvement

Germany was allied with Italy as well as Japan, which had its own ambitions to expand its influence in the Pacific. On December 7, 1941, Japan launched a surprise attack on the U.S. military base in Pearl Harbor, Hawaii.

Fact #86
★ ☆ ★

The United States joined World War II following the Japanese attack on an American naval base in Pearl Harbor, Hawaii on December 7, 1941. The United States was fighting against Japan and its allies Italy and Germany.

The United States aligned itself with Britain, France, and the Soviet Union against Japan, Italy, and Germany, who were collectively known as the Axis Powers. The war was fought in Europe, Northern Africa, and the Pacific Ocean.

Fact #87
★ ☆ ★

World War II ended in 1945 with the United States and its allies defeating the Axis Powers.

Germany surrendered to the United States and its allies in May 1945. Japan formally surrendered in September of that year, after the United States dropped two atomic bombs on Japanese cities. After the war, many countries signed peace agreements. They created the United Nations, an international organization designed to encourage international cooperation, in order to ensure there would not be another world war.

THE COLD WAR ERA

During World War II, the United States had fought alongside the Soviet Union. However, the Soviet Union's government was communist. After the war, the United States wanted to spread democracy, while the Soviet Union hoped to spread communism. For the next 50 years, both countries tried to convince other countries to adopt their ideology. Despite serious tensions, the United States and the Soviet Union never actually fought each other directly. Therefore, this period of American history is known as the Cold War.

Fact #88

★ ☆ ★

During the Cold War, the United States was concerned about the spread of communism.

Korea and Vietnam

Although the United States and the Soviet Union never fought each other directly, they did engage in several proxy wars—conflicts in other countries where the United States supported one side and the Soviet Union supported the other.

Fact #89

★ ☆ ★

The Korean War—which lasted from 1950 to 1953—was officially between North Korea and South Korea, but the United States intervened to help South Korea because North Korea was under communist influence.

During the Korean War, North Korea received help from both the Soviet Union and China, which was also communist. The United States led a group of United Nations forces in support of South Korea. The war ended in a stalemate. North Korea remained communist, but its communism did not spread to South Korea. The two countries signed an armistice, which led to the creation of a demilitarized zone along their border. However, they never signed an actual peace treaty.

Fact #90

Dwight D. Eisenhower was elected president in 1952. He previously served as a general during World War II.

Shortly after Korea, the United States engaged in another proxy war, this time in Vietnam. North Vietnam, which was communist, had support from China and the Soviet Union, while the United States supported South Vietnam.

Fact #91

★ ☆ ★

During the Vietnam War — which lasted from 1959 to 1975 — the United States helped South Vietnam against the communist North Vietnam. Nearly 60,000 American soldiers died in the war. In 1976, the communists took over all of Vietnam.

During the early 1970s, the United States began to gradually withdraw its presence in Vietnam. The war was costly and unpopular, and the American forces had not been able to stop the communist advances. The communists formally united Vietnam in 1976.

The Civil Rights Movement

While the United States grappled with communism overseas, people back at home were fighting for their basic rights. Although slavery had been abolished in 1865, African-Americans were often deprived of equal rights. In many parts of the country, they were not allowed to vote, and were forced to use separate public facilities, such as restrooms and drinking fountains.

Fact #92

The Civil Rights Movement fought against racial discrimination in the 1960s.

The Civil Rights Movement wanted to end racial inequality in the United States. People organized protests and marches for equal rights. These protests led to the passage of the Civil Rights Act in 1964 and the Voting Rights Act in 1965, which helped protect the rights of all Americans, regardless of their race.

Fact #93
★ ☆ ★

Martin Luther King, Jr. was a civil rights leader. He fought so that all Americans would be treated equally regardless of their race or economic status.

Martin Luther King Jr. was one of the most well-known civil rights leaders. He was a minister from Georgia who advocated for nonviolent protests and civil disobedience. King initially focused on racial inequality, but also argued that the United States needed to do more to support people who lived in poverty. King was assassinated in 1968.

Recent history

Since the end of the Cold War, the United States has continued to face international challenges. In 1990, the Iraq invaded Kuwait. The Kuwaiti military was unprepared, and Iraq almost immediately took control of Kuwait. The United Nations imposed sanctions on Iraq to encourage it to withdraw, but Iraq refused, so the United Nations took military action.

Fact #94
★ ☆ ★

The Persian Gulf War was fought in 1991. The United States led a group of United Nations forces which helped drive Iraqi forces from Kuwait.

After the Persian Gulf War, the United States continued to face issues in the Middle East. Many of these conflicts were with non-state actors— independent groups which are not affiliated with any particular country, but still take political action.

Fact #95
★ ☆ ★

On September 11, 2001 terrorists from the group Al-Qaeda attacked the United States. Nearly 3,000 Americans were killed.

GEOGRAPHY AND SYMBOLS

In addition to American history, people seeking naturalization are required to know about geography and national symbols. This next section will address the geography and symbols that come up on the citizenship test.

Rivers and oceans

The United States is home to thousands of rivers and lakes. Many of these bodies of water are economically important or have significance in their local communities. However, for the purposes of becoming a citizen, people only need to know about the most important bodies of water.

Fact #96
★ ☆ ★

The Missouri River is the longest river in the United States. It starts in the mountains of Montana and eventually flows into the Mississippi River.

The song "America the Beautiful" says that the country stretches from "sea to shining sea." The seas referenced in the song are actually oceans. The United States technically borders three oceans, as Alaska borders the Arctic Ocean.

Fact #97

★ ☆ ★

The West Coast of the United States borders the Pacific Ocean, while the East Coast borders the Atlantic Ocean.

States and territories

Over the course of American history, the United States has possessed a lot of territories. Some of these territories, such as Hawaii, became states. Others, such as the Philippines, became their own countries. Today, the United States has five major territories.

Fact #98

★ ☆ ★

There are five major U.S. territories: Puerto Rico, the U.S. Virgin Islands, American Samoa, the Northern Mariana Islands, and Guam.

When the United States was founded, early politicians did not want to put the capital city in any state, because they feared that doing so would give a particular state too much power. Today, the capital city still remains its own district.

Fact #99

★ ☆ ★

Washington D.C. is the capital of the United States. It is not part of any state.

Borders

The United States borders Canada and Mexico. Canada is located north of the United States. Its border with the United States is about 5,524 miles long. Mexico is located south of the United States. Its border with the United States is about 1,954 miles long.

Fact #100

★ ☆ ★

Thirteen U.S. states border Canada. They are: Alaska, Washington, Idaho, Montana, North Dakota, Minnesota, Michigan, Ohio, Pennsylvania, New York, Vermont, New Hampshire, and Maine.

Fact #101

★ ☆ ★

Four U.S. states border Mexico. They are: California, Arizona, New Mexico, and Texas.

Songs, symbols, and statues

Many symbols represent the United States. Some of these symbols are designed to encourage patriotism; others emphasize important American values. The citizenship test requires individuals to know about a few of these symbols.

Fact #102

★ ☆ ★

The American flag has 13 red and white stripes to represent the 13 original colonies. It has 50 stars to represent the 50 states.

The American flag is probably the most recognizable symbol of the United States. The flag also served as inspiration for the national anthem. During the War of 1812, poet Francis Scott Key was inspired by watching the flag wave during the Battle of Baltimore. Key wrote a poem called "The Star-Spangled Banner," which later was adapted into the national anthem.

Fact #103

★ ☆ ★

The Star-Spangled Banner is the national anthem of the
United States.

Many people find it difficult to sing the national anthem. However, it is
fairly easy to say the Pledge of Allegiance. When individuals say the Pledge,
they assert their allegiance to the flag, and to the United States.

Fact #104

★ ☆ ★

The Pledge of Allegiance was first recognized by
Congress in 1942. People typically say the pledge while
facing an American flag and holding their right hand
over their heart.

The Pledge of Allegiance goes: "I pledge Allegiance to the flag of the United States of America, and to the Republic for which it stands, one nation under God, indivisible, with Liberty and Justice for all."

The Statue of Liberty

The Statue of Liberty is an essential American symbol. France gave the statue to the United States in 1886 as a recognition of the alliance between the two countries. The statue is meant to represent freedom and democracy.

Fact #105

★ ☆ ★

The Statue of Liberty resides on Liberty Island in New York Harbor.

The Statue of Liberty also has meaning for many immigrants to the United States. New York has often been a destination for immigrants, and the statue was one of the first sights that many immigrants saw when they arrived by boat.

Fact #106

★ ☆ ★

The Statue of Liberty is visible from Ellis Island,
where millions of immigrants from Europe passed
through during the 1800s and 1900s.

Holidays

To recognize important events and people, the United States recognizes certain days as federal holidays. On these days, non-essential government workers receive the day off from work, and many private employers also give their workers the day off.

Fact #107

★ ☆ ★

The United States celebrates 10 federal holidays, many
of which honor important people or events in
American history.

The 10 federal holidays are: New Year's Day, the Birthday of Martin Luther King, Jr., President's Day, Memorial Day, Independence Day, Labor Day, Columbus Day, Veterans Day, Thanksgiving Day, and Christmas Day.

This chapter has addressed many of the topics that are covered on the citizenship exam — topics that every American should know and understand. The next chapter will address another essential topic: The U.S. Constitution.

CHAPTER 7

Understanding the Constitution

The naturalization process requires individuals who want to become citizens to have good understanding of the U.S. Constitution. This chapter will explain the principles of the Constitution, so that new citizens can pass their citizenship test and understand the country they are becoming a part of.

Fact #108

★ ☆ ★

The Constitution is often described as the "supreme law of the land." It outlines the principles of the U.S. government and the rights of all Americans.

No one in the United States is above the law. The Constitution describes the powers of the government as well as its limitations. The Founding Fathers wanted to ensure that the new American government would not become tyrannical, like the British government had been.

Fact #109

★ ☆ ★

The Constitution establishes the rule of law for the United States. Everyone must follow the law, including everyday citizens, leaders, and the government.

PARTS OF THE CONSTITUTION

Fact #110

★ ☆ ★

The Constitution is composed of the preamble, seven articles, and the amendments.

The Constitution can be divided into three basic parts. The first part, the Preamble, is the introduction to the Constitution. The Preamble explains why the Founding Fathers chose to write the Constitution.

Fact #111

★ ☆ ★

The Preamble to the Constitution beings with the words "We the People." These words establish the idea of popular sovereignty—that the power to govern comes from the people.

The Preamble is followed by the articles of the Constitution. The articles describe the structure of the government, including the different parts of the federal government and the relationship between the federal government and the states. Finally, the amendments describe the rights of citizens and make some changes to the original Constitution.

Fact #112

★ ☆ ★

Amendments change or add to the Constitution. Over the course of U.S. history, there have been 27 amendments.

Articles of the Constitution

Under the Articles of Confederation, the United States had been disorganized and divided. When the Founding Fathers were writing the Constitution, they knew they needed to create a stronger central government. However, they did not want to give too much power to any person.

Fact #113

★ ☆ ★

The first three articles of the Constitution designate the three branches of government.

To make sure that power was not too concentrated, the Founding Fathers divided the federal government into three parts. Each of these parts was given separate powers and duties. Additionally, the Constitution established a system of checks and balances. Each branch of government can check each other's powers, which creates a balance.

Fact #114

★ ☆ ★

The Founding Fathers established these separate branches of government to ensure no one part would become too powerful. This system is known as separation of powers or checks and balances.

For example, Congress, part of the legislative branch, can pass a law, but it must be signed by the president, who is part of the executive branch. Even if both the president and Congress agree on a law, a court in the judicial branch still has the power to declare the law unconstitutional. If that seems confusing, don't worry! The next few sections—and most of Chapter 8—will explain the different functions of government and how laws are created.

Article I

The first article of the Constitution describes the legislative branch. The legislative branch is responsible for passing laws and is made up of the two houses of Congress—the House of Representatives and the Senate.

Fact #115

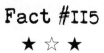

Article I of the Constitution outlines the powers and limitations of Congress.

When the Founding Fathers were writing the Constitution, they disagreed over the structure of the legislative branch. Some people thought that each state should get the same number of representatives in Congress. Others argued that states with more people should get more representatives.

Fact #116

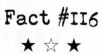

The two houses of Congress (the Senate and House of Representatives) exist because of a plan known as the Connecticut Compromise.

Two representatives from Connecticut, Roger Sherman and Oliver Ellsworth, proposed a compromise. They suggested a bicameral legislature, meaning that the legislative branch would have two chambers. One of the chambers would have representatives allocated by population, and one would have representatives allocated equally to each state.

As a result of the Connecticut Compromise, representatives in the House of Representatives are distributed based on the population of each state, whereas each state elects two senators, regardless of its population.

Fact #II7

★ ☆ ★

According to the original Constitution, senators were not elected by the people, but by state legislatures. The I7th Amendment would change this process.

The Founding Fathers did not trust average people to elect strong candidates to government. Therefore, the Constitution originally stated that senators would be elected by state legislatures, not everyday citizens. This would change with the passage of the 17th Amendment in 1913.

Fact #II8

★ ☆ ★

Article I also declares that certain powers are enumerated—given—to the federal government. These powers include the ability to print money, to declare war, to raise an army, and to sign treaties with foreign countries.

The first article of the Constitution also outlines some of the specific functions of the legislative branch. Congress has the power tax, spend, borrow, and print money; it can regulate commerce and establish policies about bankruptcy and naturalization; it can build Post Offices, come up with copyright and patent laws; it can create courts; it can build an army and declare war. These responsibilities are known as the enumerated powers.

Articles II-VII
The second article of the Constitution outlines the structure of the executive branch. The executive branch is led by the president. The president appoints a cabinet—a group of advisers who lead different departments and give the president advice.

Fact #119

Article II of the Constitution outlines the powers and limitations of the president.

According to Article II, the vice president serves as president if the president is unable to fulfill his duties. The original Constitution stated that the vice president would be whoever received the second-most votes in the presidential election, but this was later changed.

Fact #120

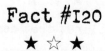

Article III of the Constitution discusses the Supreme Court.

Article III of the Constitution established the Supreme Court as the highest court in the United States. Congress, according to Article I, was given the power to make lower courts. Today, the role of the Supreme Court is to determine the constitutionality of laws. However, the original Constitution did not specify this power—judges later decided that it was the Supreme Court's job.

Fact #121

Article IV of the Constitution discusses the relations between states.

The Founding Fathers wanted to ensure that Americans citizens would be treated equally, regardless of where they were from. Article IV of the Constitution requires states to honor each other's "public Acts, records, and judicial proceedings." The article also declares that citizens from any state are still entitled the protections and privileges in other states.

Article IV also established that new states which joined the country would be on "equal footing" with states that were already a part of the United States. Vermont became the first state to join the country (after the 13 original states) in 1791.

Fact #122

★ ☆ ★

Article V of the Constitution explains how the Constitution can be amended.

The Founding Fathers recognized that the Constitution was not perfect. Amendments, as outlined by Article V, allowed for changes to the Constitution. Although there are multiple ways to pass an amendment, only one has ever been used. For an amendment to be passed, is must be approved by a two-thirds margin in both the Senate and the House of Representatives, and then receive approval in three-fourths of state legislatures.

Fact #123
★ ☆ ★

Article VI of the Constitution includes the supremacy clause. This clause states that the Constitution and other federal laws overrule state and local laws.

The supremacy clause established a clear distinction between the Articles of Confederation—under which the federal government was weak—and the Constitution. Article VI also states that there cannot be a religious test as a requirement for holding public office, meaning that people can work for the government regardless of their religion.

Fact #124
★ ☆ ★

Article VII of the Constitution stated that the Constitution would go into effect once nine of the 13 original states ratified it.

The Constitution was signed in September 1787, but it could not take effect until three-fourths of the states approved it. This happened on June 21, 1788, when New Hampshire became the ninth state to ratify it.

The Bill of Rights

When the Constitution was written, some people objected to it, because it did not discuss the rights and protections for citizens. The first 10 amendments were written to address this concern. They are known as the Bill of Rights.

Fact #125

★ ☆ ★

While the Constitution was signed in 1787, the Bill of Rights—the first 10 amendments—was not finalized until 1792.

Rights and freedoms

The first three amendments address the rights of all citizens. Many of the rights protected by these amendments are rights that the colonists felt the British had violated leading up to the Revolutionary War.

Fact #126

★ ☆ ★

The First Amendment guarantees five fundamental
rights: freedom of religion, freedom of speech, freedom
of assembly, freedom of the press, and freedom to
petition the government.

Many of the first settlers of the United States were seeking to avoid persecution because of their religious beliefs. Therefore, freedom of religion was
the first freedom listed in the Bill of Rights. The other four freedoms in the
First Amendment aimed to ensure the people could speak up against the
government.

Fact #127

★ ☆ ★

The Second Amendment guarantees the right to bear arms
in order to create a well-regulated militia.

The Second Amendment guarantees the right to bear arms, which refers to the
right of individual citizens to own weapons. The limitations on the Second
Amendment have been the subject of much debate over the last century.

Fact #128

★ ☆ ★

The Third Amendment says that individuals cannot be
required to quarter soldiers.

Today, the Third Amendment seems pretty irrelevant. However, at the time
it was written, it was essential: During the Revolutionary War, many colo-

nists had been forced to provide shelter to British soldiers. The Founding Fathers wanted to make sure this would never happen in the United States.

Crime and punishment

Several amendments in the Bill of Rights address crime and due process. These amendments are designed to make sure that people who are accused of a crime are treated fairly, and that people who are convicted of a crime receive an appropriate punishment.

Fact #129
★ ☆ ★

The Fourth Amendment protects individuals from "unreasonable searches and seizures." It effectively means that police must have a good reason—and a warrant from a judge—before they look through someone's home or belongings.

Because of the Fourth Amendment, law enforcement agencies are required to get a warrant signed by a judge before they search a person. To obtain a warrant, the agency must prove that there is "probable cause" that an individual committed a crime. Evidence obtained without a warrant is considered inadmissible in court—it cannot be used against someone.

Fact #130
★ ☆ ★

The Fifth Amendment addresses the rights of people accused of a crime. It includes the principle of no "double jeopardy"—no one can be tried for the same crime twice.

The Fifth Amendment also includes the provision that people cannot be forced to testify against themselves in court. This principle has led to the saying, "I plead the Fifth"—which is what someone might say to avoid tell self-incriminating information.

Fact #131

★ ☆ ★

The Sixth Amendment guarantees people accused of a crime the right to a speedy trial.

Although the Sixth Amendment guarantees the right to a speedy trial, it does not define what qualifies as "speedy." The Supreme Court has not established a set time within which a trial must occur; instead, it came up with a set of criteria to determine whether a trial is speedy on a case-by-case basis. The Sixth Amendment also states that people who are accused of a crime have the right to a trial by an "impartial jury."

Fact #132

★ ☆ ★

The Seventh Amendment guarantees individuals the right to a jury trial in civil cases—legal disputes where no crime has been committed—if at least $20 is at stake.

While the previous amendments address people accused of a crime, the Seventh Amendment addresses civil cases. In civil cases, the plaintiff (the person who brings the lawsuit) typically asks for money from the defendant (the person who they are suing) because of something that the defendant has done.

The Seventh Amendment gave the right to jury trials for civil cases where "the value in controversy shall exceed twenty dollars." While this number has not changed despite inflation—people are still allowed to sue in court for any amount over $20—many people choose to resolve their controversies in other ways.

Fact #133

The Eighth Amendment prohibits cruel and unusual punishment.

As with previous amendments, the Eighth Amendment bans "cruel and unusual punishments," but does not define which punishments are cruel and unusual. The Supreme Court has ruled, in various cases, that the Eighth Amendment forbids certain punishments in all circumstances, and bans other punishments that are cruel and unusual in comparison to the crime that a person committed.

Other rights

Although the first eight amendments address many rights, they are not an all-inclusive list. The Ninth Amendment acknowledges that the Constitution does not include all the rights that American citizens possess, while the Tenth Amendment addresses the balance of powers between states and the federal government.

Fact #134

★ ☆ ★

The Ninth Amendment states that the rights not mentioned in the Constitution are still "retained by the people."

Some of the Founding Fathers were concerned that, if the government listed certain rights, then people might think that these were the only rights that citizens possessed. The Ninth Amendment clarifies that people still have other rights, in addition to those outlined in the Constitution.

Fact #135

★ ☆ ★

The Tenth Amendment says that powers not discussed in the Constitution belong to the states.

The powers that belong to states, according to the Tenth Amendment, include powers that the Founding Fathers could not have imagined. For example, states have the power to issue drivers licenses. They also have the power to create police departments and public schools—none of which are mentioned in the Constitution.

Amendments 11-27

While the first 10 amendments were intended to outline the rights of citizens, many of the amendments since then were written to modify specific portions of the Constitution. The 11th Amendment, ratified in 1795, addressed concerns about how states could be sued.

Fact #136

★ ☆ ★

The 11th Amendment limits some of the ways states can be sued in federal court.

The original Constitution said that the runner-up in the presidential election would become the vice president. But Thomas Jefferson, who was elected president in 1800, didn't get along well with his runner-up, Vice President Aaron Burr. Thus, the amendment was passed in 1804 to change the selection process for vice president.

Fact #137
★ ☆ ★

The 12th Amendment established that the president and the vice president would run for office together, on a single ticket.

Post-Civil War amendments

After the Civil War, the United States passed a series of amendments to end slavery and grant African-Americans equal rights. Southern states were required to ratify these amendments in order to rejoin the country.

Fact #138
★ ☆ ★

The 13th Amendment, ratified in 1865, abolished slavery, except as punishment for a crime.

While ending slavery was certainly consequential, the 13th Amendment has rarely been cited in court cases since its passage. By contrast, the 14th Amendment — which had five clauses — has been cited in many cases, and remains relevant today.

Fact #139

★ ☆ ★

The 14th Amendment was ratified in 1868. It includes the
equal protection clause, which remains highly
relevant—and up for interpretation—today. This clause
says that no state can deprive any person "the equal
protection the laws."

As discussed in Chapter 2, the 14th Amendment also declared that anyone who was born in the United States was automatically a citizen. The 14th Amendment also stated that no state could "deprive any person of life, liberty, or property, without due process of law." This clause, which is similar to the Fifth Amendment, was especially intended to ensure that Southern states did not violate the rights of their African-American citizens.

Fact #140

★ ☆ ★

Ratified in 1870, the 15th Amendment declared that
people of all races can vote.

The 15th Amendment declared that a person could not be denied the right to vote solely on the basis of their race. Although the amendment was designed to ensure that African-American men could vote, many states initially used other mechanisms, such as literacy tests, to prevent former slaves from voting.

20th century amendments

Fact #141

★ ☆ ★

The 16th Amendment, ratified in 1913, gives Congress the
power to tax income.

Prior to the 16th Amendment, Congress mostly raised revenue by taxing specific goods. In 1894, the Supreme Court ruled a particular income tax to be unconstitutional. However, many progressives in the early 1900s thought that an income tax would be a good idea, so they passed the amendment.

Fact #142
★ ☆ ★

The 17th Amendment established that Senators were elected by popular vote—the system that remains in place today.

Until the ratification of the 17th Amendment in 1913, Senators were chosen by state legislatures. In addition to making senators elected by popular vote, the amendment also allowed state governors to appoint senators temporarily in the event of a vacancy.

Fact #143
★ ☆ ★

The 18th Amendment, known as prohibition, banned all sales of alcohol in the United States. It was ratified in 1919.

During the early 20th century, many people began to see alcohol as a social problem. As a result, the 18th Amendment was passed, banning the sales of alcohol in the entire country.

Fact #144

The 19th Amendment, ratified in 1920, guaranteed women
the right to vote.

Women achieved the right to vote in 1920 due to the 19th Amendment.
Although some states already allowed women the right to vote, the amendment established voting rights for women nationally.

Fact #145

★ ☆ ★

The 20th Amendment, ratified in 1933 under President
Franklin D. Roosevelt, moved up the inauguration date
for the new president from March to January.

Under the original Constitution, a president who was elected in November would not take office until January. This time period was designed to ensure that the president had enough time to transition into the new office. However, improvements in communication and transportation technology made this transition period excessively long.

The amendment also stipulates that if something happens to the president-elect between the election and inauguration day, the vice president-elect will become president. This provision was relevant because Roosevelt suffered an assassination attempt in February 1933, prior to his inauguration.

Fact #146
★ ☆ ★

The 21st Amendment repealed the 18th Amendment, and therefore allowed the sale of alcohol once again. It was ratified in 1933.

Prohibition, the ban on alcohol resulting from the 18th Amendment, did not have the effects that people had hoped it would. During the 1920s, many people continued to consume alcohol illegally. Furthermore, the government lost the tax revenue it had once gained from legal sales of alcohol. As a result, states agreed to repeal the 18th Amendment by passing the 21st Amendment.

Fact #147

The 22nd Amendment, ratified in 1951, limited presidents from serving more than two terms.

Since President George Washington had chosen to retire after serving two terms, every American president had followed his lead. However, President Roosevelt decided to reverse this trend by running for reelection in 1940 after he had already served two terms. Although Roosevelt won reelection in both 1940 and 1944—meaning he was elected president four times— people decided afterward to formally ban presidents from being president for more than two terms.

Fact #148

★ ☆ ★

Until the 23rd Amendment was ratified in 1961, people living in Washington D.C. could not vote in presidential elections. This amendment granted them three electoral votes.

The Founding Fathers established Washington D.C., the capital, as its own separate district—not a part of any state—in order to ensure that no state would be too powerful. However, this posed a problem for people living in the city, as they could not vote in presidential elections. The 23rd Amendment resolved this issue.

Fact #149

★ ☆ ★

The 24th Amendment, ratified in 1964, banned poll taxes.

Prior to the 24th Amendment, five states implemented poll taxes—a fee that citizens had to pay in order to vote. Poll taxes often discouraged poor people from voting. Thus, the amendment was designed to make voting more accessible to all citizens.

Fact #150

★ ☆ ★

The 25th Amendment clarified the procedure of presidential succession — what happens if the president dies or otherwise becomes incapacitated. It was ratified in 1967.

Although the Constitution said that the vice president would take the president's position if the president was unable to serve, it did not say for how long the vice president would serve, and it did not say who would become vice president. After President John F. Kennedy was assassinated in 1963, President Lyndon B. Johnson served as president for over a year without a vice president.

The 25th Amendment also provides that the president can temporarily yield power to the vice president. Both Presidents Ronald Reagan and

George H.W. Bush invoked the 25th Amendment to temporarily transfer power to their vice presidents while they underwent surgeries.

Fact #151
★ ☆ ★

The 26th Amendment, ratified in 1971, lowered the voting age from 21 to 18.

During the 1960s, many young men were drafted into the military to fight in the Vietnam War. Since men could be drafted at age 18, many people argued that it was unfair to send people to war who were not old enough to vote. The 26th Amendment resolved this issue by lowering the vote age.

Fact #152
★ ☆ ★

The 27th Amendment prevents Congress from voting itself an immediate pay raise.

The 27th Amendment followed a unique path. It was initially submitted to the states for ratification in 1789, along with 11 other amendments. Ten of those amendments were passed and became the Bill of Rights. The 27th Amendment was mostly forgotten, but in 1982, a student named Gregory Watson who attended the University of Texas at Austin, wrote a research paper about it. Watson ended up starting a push to ratify the amendment. By 1992, enough states ratified the amendment, so it took effect—203 years after it was initially proposed.

CHAPTER 8

Understanding American Government

The Constitution, as discussed last chapter, outlines the structure of the U.S. government. However, the Constitution alone does not provide a complete understanding of how the government really functions today. For example, the Constitution granted Congress the power to create courts — the existence of these courts and how they function has changed a lot in the last 200 years!

Furthermore, the Constitution doesn't mention anything about political parties, even though they play an important role in American politics. Likewise, many government functions — such as regulating airplanes or issuing drivers' licenses — were not relevant when the Constitution was written. These functions of government have evolved over time.

This chapter will address the way the U.S. government functions today. All citizens — born or naturalized — have the obligation to be informed about American politics, as everyone plays a role in shaping the country's future.

THE THREE BRANCHES OF GOVERNMENT

As outlined by the Constitution, the federal government of the United States is divided into three branches. (The federal government refers to the national government). Individual states also have their own governments, which also have three branches.

Each branch of government serves a different function. The legislative branch is responsible for passing laws; the executive branch enforces these laws; the judicial branch ensures that the laws are applied equally and follow the principles of the Constitution. However, government is a bit more complicated than just these basic functions. The next few sections will address the different jobs belonging to each branch.

The legislative branch

As discussed last chapter, the legislative branch is made up of the two houses of Congress, the House of Representatives, and the Senate. Members of Congress propose bills, which are potential laws.

Fact #153

★ ☆ ★

Members of either chamber of Congress can propose a
bill; if both chambers approve it, it goes to the
president for consideration.

Although the legislative branch is responsible for passing laws, the president also gets to make a decision. This reflects the system of checks and balances. As part of the executive branch, the president must cooperate with the legislative branch.

Fact #154

★ ☆ ★

The president has the power to sign bills into laws, or veto them.

However, the president does not have absolute power when it comes to vetoing bills. If members of Congress really like a bill, they can override the president's veto if they get enough votes.

Fact #155

★ ☆ ★

The Senate and the House can override a president's veto if both houses have two-thirds majority in favor of a bill the president has vetoed.

The House of Representatives

The House of Representatives is the lower of the two houses of Congress. States send representatives to the House based on their populations. To elect representatives, states are divided into Congressional districts. People living in a given Congressional district elect their representative.

Fact #156
★ ☆ ★

Alaska, Delaware, Montana, North Dakota, South Dakota, Vermont and Wyoming only send one representative to the House, while California has 53 Congressional districts and therefore sends 53 representatives to the House.

Since the House of Representatives is based on state population, the number of representatives in the House has changed over time, because the number of people living in the United States has grown and new states have joined.

To represent a Congressional District as a member of the House of Representatives, a person must be living in that district. Members of the House must fulfill a few other requirements — they must be at least 25 years old, and have been a citizen of the United States for at least seven years.

Fact #157
★ ☆ ★

When the first House of Representatives met, it had 59 members. Today, it has 435 voting members.

Representatives from each of the 50 states are known as voting members. These representatives can propose bills and vote. The House also has non-voting members, who represent U.S. territories.

Fact #158
★ ☆ ★

U.S. territories, such as American Samoa and Guam, elect honorary members to the House of Representatives. These representatives give speeches and discuss issues, but they cannot vote.

Members of the House of Representatives are supposed to represent their constituents—the people who elected them to office. To make sure that representatives are listening to voters, elections for the House are held in every state every two years. If representatives want to get reelected, they must listen to their constituents.

Fact #159
★ ☆ ★

Members of the House of Representatives are elected every two years.

There is no term limit for members of the national House of Representatives, which means that representatives can serve for as many two-year terms as they want—assuming they keep winning elections! Some state houses of representatives do have term limits.

435 members is a lot! To help with organization, members of the House elect a speaker, who is responsible for leading the House. Typically, the Speaker of the House is from whichever political party has a majority. The

Speaker of the House is responsible for negotiating between political parties and bringing bills to a vote. The role of political parties will be discussed later in this chapter.

Fact #160
★ ☆ ★

Members of the House elect the Speaker of the House
every two years. The speaker of the house presides over
the House of Representatives.

The Senate
The Senate is the upper chamber of Congress. While the House has 435 members, the Senate only has 100 — so senators are generally considered more powerful than representatives. Senators must be residents of the state that they represent. Additionally, senators must be at least 30 years old and have been a U.S. citizen for at least nine years.

Each state elects two senators. As a result, there have always been an even number of senators, no matter how the number of states. As a result, Senate votes sometimes results in ties. To resolve this issue, the vice president serves as the tiebreaking vote in the Senate.

Fact #161
★ ☆ ★

The vice president officially presides over the Senate,
and would serve as the deciding vote in the event
of a tie.

The vice president is technically a member of the executive branch. Therefore, the role that the vice president also plays in the Senate is another example of checks and balances—the ways in which different parts of government keep tabs on each other's powers.

Fact #162

★ ☆ ★

Senators serve six-year terms.

Like members of the House of Representatives, senators do not have term limits. The longest serving center ever was Robert C. Byrd, a democratic senator from West Virginia who held the position for 51 years!

Who represents you?

Fact #163

★ ☆ ★

The Citizenship Test makes ask individuals to name their senators and representatives, as well as the current president and vice president of the United States.

Individuals are required to know their elected officials in order to pass the citizenship test, but all Americans should learn who their senators and representatives are. Websites like **http://www.house.gov/representatives/find/** and **http://whoismyrepresentative.com/** allow citizens to look up representatives and senators.

The executive branch

The executive branch is led by the president. The president is generally considered the most powerful politician in the United States—after all, there is only one president, compared to 100 senators and 435 representatives.

Fact #164

★ ☆ ★

The president must be a natural-born citizen of the
United States, at least 35 years of age, and have resided
in the country for at least 14 years.

Because the president is the highest position in government, the requirements to become president are very stringent. Most notably, the president must be a natural born citizen—which means that individuals who immigrate to the United States and become naturalized citizens cannot run for president.

Fact #165

★ ☆ ★

The president is elected every four years.

Presidential elections are held every four years. Today, presidents are allowed to hold two terms, or eight total years, in office. If the current president runs for reelection after one term, he or she is known as the incumbent.

Fact #166

★ ☆ ★

Presidential elections always take place on the first Tuesday after the first Monday in November.

Due to a law passed in 1845, presidential elections take place on the first Tuesday after the first Monday in November every four years. When there is not a presidential election, local elections often still take place in November, but some special elections are held at other times during the year.

The president's roles
This chapter already discussed one of the president's key roles—signing (or vetoing) bills passed by Congress. With the help of advisors, the president also makes many other decisions independent of Congress.

Fact #167

★ ☆ ★

The president serves as the Commander in Chief of the military.

The president is in charge of the military, which means deciding where to station troops and how to use weapons. As part of the system of checks and balances, only Congress can declare war, but the president can still use the military, even if the United States is not in an official war. In fact, Congress has not officially declared war since 1941, when it declared war against

Japan during World War II, even though the country has been in many conflicts since.

Fact #168

★ ☆ ★

The president appoints a cabinet, which is a group of advisers.

The president has to make a lot of very important decisions, but the president cannot be an expert on every single subject! Instead, the president is surrounded by a group of advisers known as the cabinet. Members of the cabinet oversee special government agencies.

The president gets to appoint members of cabinet, but the Senate must approve them. There are currently 15 cabinet positions. The oldest — the Secretary of State and the Secretary of the Treasury — were created in 1789. The Secretary of Homeland Security, the newest cabinet position, was established in 2002.

Fact #169

★ ☆ ★

New cabinet positions have been added over time.

The complete list of cabinet positions are: the Secretary of State, the Secretary of the Treasury, the Secretary of Defense, the Attorney General, the Secretary of the Interior, the Secretary of Agriculture, the Secretary of Commerce, the Secretary of Labor, the Secretary of Health and Human Services, the Secretary of Housing and Urban Development, the Secretary of Transportation, the Secretary of Energy, the Secretary of Education, the Secretary of Veterans Affairs, and the Secretary of Homeland Security.

Presidential succession

At times in American history, the president has been unable to serve, as a result of illness or death. As discussed last chapter, the vice president immediately becomes president if something happens to the president. However, there is actually a long line of presidential succession — people who could potentially become president in the event of a catastrophe.

Fact #170
★ ☆ ★

If both the president and vice president are unable to serve, the Speaker of the House becomes president.

The Speaker of the House is third in the line of presidential succession. After the Speaker of the House, the Senate majority leader — someone who is elected by whichever political party has the most senators — would become president. After the Senate majority leader, members of the president's cabinet would become president, beginning with the Secretary of State.

Fact #171
★ ☆ ★

If the president, vice president, and Speaker of the House are all unable to serve, the Senate majority leader would become president, followed by members of the president's cabinet.

It is very unlikely that something bad would happen to the president, the vice president, the Speaker of the House, the Senate majority leader, and the members of the president's cabinet. However, to avoid the possibility that an attack could leave the American government without a president, cabinet members take turns sitting out on major presidential speeches.

The judicial branch

When the Founding Fathers wrote the Constitution, they only established the Supreme Court, and gave Congress the power to create all lower courts. The judiciary refers the entire system of courts in the United States.

Fact #172
★ ☆ ★

The Supreme Court is the highest court in the United States, while the judiciary includes lower courts, which are established by Congress.

Within the federal courts system, there are 12 appellate courts below the Supreme Court. These courts hear appeals from the 94 district courts located across the country. Some district courts deal only with special matters, such as bankruptcy or trade. States also have their own court systems.

Fact #173

★ ☆ ★

There are nine justices on the Supreme Court.

The Constitution didn't specify how many justices would be on the Supreme Court. In 1789, Congress passed a law calling for a Chief Justice and five other justices. Over the years, various other laws changed this number. However, Congress passed another law in 1869 calling for nine total justices on the Supreme Court, the number that remains today.

With nine justices, the Supreme Court issues rulings on a majority basis. If five or more justices vote to uphold a law, then it will be upheld; if five or more vote that a law is unconstitutional, then the law will be declared unconstitutional. However, in certain circumstances, a tie can occur on the Supreme Court. For example, if a justice dies and the court must rule on cases before a new justice is appointed, the court will only have eight justices and some cases may result in ties. If a Supreme Court vote results in a tie, then the ruling of the lower court—the court that heard the case right before it reached the Supreme Court—will stand.

Fact #174

★ ☆ ★

Justices on the Supreme Court are appointed by the president and must be confirmed by the Senate.

The process for appointing Supreme Court nominees is an example of the system of checks and balances. The president, a member of the executive branch, nominates a judge to the Supreme Court. The Senate, part of the legislative branch, must confirm the nominee by voting in their favor.

Fact #175

★ ☆ ★

Supreme Court justices are appointed for life.

Elected officials in the United States serve for a certain period of time—for example, members of the House of Representatives serve two-year terms, senators serve six-year terms, and the president serves four-year terms. Supreme Court justices, unlike other officials, serve until they die or choose to step down.

Why are Supreme Court justices treated differently from other federal officials? The Founding Fathers wanted to ensure judicial independence from the political system. While the president and members of Congress often make decisions based on their opinions, or the opinions of their constituents, members of the Supreme Court are supposed to follow and interpret the Constitution. Since justices don't have to worry about reelection, they can make unpopular decisions.

Fact #176

★ ☆ ★

The Constitution does not mention the power of the Supreme Court to declare laws unconstitutional. The 1803 court case *Marbury v. Madison* established this power.

Although the Supreme Court first met in 1789, it did not actually declare a law unconstitutional until 1803. Initially, the court simply judged whether an individual had been wronged, or whether a law had been interpreted correctly. But in the decision for *Marbury v. Madison*, Chief Justice

John Marshall found that a law—the Judiciary Act of 1789—conflicted with parts of the Constitution, and therefore could not continue to be law.

Fact #177
★ ☆ ★

The Supreme Court has the power to overrule state and federal courts.

As its name implies (and the Constitution dictates), the Supreme Court is the nation's highest court. This means that the Supreme Court never takes cases right away. Instead, most cases are resolved by state or district courts. However, if one side challenges a court's ruling, the case might proceed to a higher court—eventually reaching the Supreme Court, who has the final ruling.

POLITICS AND PARTIES

Anyone who reads about American politics today probably hears a lot about political parties. Unlike political offices, parties are not officially part of the structure of the government, and they were not mentioned in the Constitution. However, parties play an important role in how the government functions today.

Fact #178
★ ☆ ★

In his farewell address delivered in 1796, George Washington—the first president of the United States— warned against political parties, arguing that they would work in their own best interests, rather than that of the country.

Political parties are groups of individuals with similar ideas or goals. People form parties in order to increase their chances of winning elections. For example, say that raising taxes was a big issue in a particular district. In the district election, one candidate ran promising to raise taxes, while five candidates ran promising to lower taxes. If 40 percent of district residents want to raise taxes, while 60 percent want to lower taxes then the candidate who promised to raise taxes might get 40 percent of the vote, while the candidates promising to lower taxes might each get just 12 percent of the vote. In this scenario, the candidate who promised to raise taxes wins, even though the majority of voters supported other candidates.

Fact #179

Major parties hold primary elections or caucuses, where members of the party decide on the candidate the party will put forward for the general election.

Political parties resolve this problem by allowing individuals with similar ideas to rally around a single candidate. Parties decide on their candidates at caucuses, meetings where party members gather and vote, or during primary elections, where party members vote on a candidate like they would in a real election.

Fact #180

The political parties in the United States have changed over time. For instance, in the 1800s, the Whigs were a major party.

Parties today

Despite President Washington's warning, the United States has had political parties for most of its history. The names and ideologies of these parties have changed over time, but the government has typically been dominated by exactly two parties.

Fact #181

★ ☆ ★

The United States currently has two major political parties: the Republicans and the Democrats.

While the Republicans and Democrats are major political parties, regular citizens can also be Republicans or Democrats. Involvement with a political party is one way for Americans to participate in democracy. Individuals who choose to belong to a political party usually have the right to vote in its primary elections or participate in its caucuses.

Fact #182
★ ☆ ★

Voters can register as a member of a party, or register
as an independent voter.

Some citizens prefer not to affiliate with a major party. They can choose to register as an independent voter (meaning they are not affiliated with any political party) or as a member of a smaller party.

Fact #183
★ ☆ ★

There are many smaller parties in American politics,
such as the Green Party and the Libertarian Party.

STATE AND LOCAL GOVERNMENTS

Most of this chapter has focused on the federal government—the people who meet in Washington D.C. and decide the country's highest laws. Although the federal government may be the highest form of government (remember the supremacy clause!), state and local governments still create important laws that impact people's lives.

The structure of government

Fact #184
★ ☆ ★

State governments are typically structured similar to
the federal government. State legislatures draft bills,
and state governors have the power to sign or veto them.
States also have their own supreme courts.

Although state governments are set up similarly to the federal governments, states have their own responsibilities. For example, while the federal government is primarily responsible for providing national defense, states are primarily responsible for providing public schools.

Fact #185

States have their own constitutions.

Just as the United States has a Constitution, each state has its own constitution. However, many state constitutions serve a different purpose from the national Constitution. While the Constitution declared the basic rights and principles that define American government, state constitutions often deal with more specific policy issues.

Local governments

Fact #186

★ ☆ ★

Local governments, such as town councils, also create rules and laws.

Below the state level, local governments operate within counties, cities and towns. Many local officials—like county clerks or town council members—are elected, but these local governments operate quite differently from the state and federal governments. For example, town councils often make decisions on local matters by a majority vote among town council members. Other local officials, such as district attorneys, are elected, but have free reign to do their jobs once they take office.

Fact #187

★ ☆ ★

State and local elections are held even in years where
there is no presidential election.

Although the presidential election is only held every four years, local elections are typically held every year. Many local elections are held in November, but elections can also be held at other times of the year — it is important to stay informed!

In addition to voting for elected officials, local elections often include ballot questions or referendums. These measures ask voters to decide on a specific question. For example, should a town impose a five-cent fee on plastic bags? Should a state outlaw the death penalty? While these questions could be resolved by a town council or a state legislature, elected officials sometimes leave these decision up to the voters.

In conclusion

This chapter has addressed the basic principles and functions of American government, at the local, state, and federal levels. Along with an understanding of the U.S. Constitution (Chapter 7) and American history (Chapter 6), the information in this chapter provides the necessary knowledge for individuals to pass the citizenship test. The next chapter will address the details of the test itself—and the final steps for soon-to-be citizens!

CHAPTER 9

The Citizenship Test

The citizenship test is the final stage in the naturalization process. Individuals take the citizenship test during their interview with a USCIS official. The test is composed of two parts—a civics test, which addresses American history, geography, and government, and the English test, which assesses applicants' proficiency in speaking, reading, and writing English.

Fact #188

★ ☆ ★

According to USCIS, approximately 91 percent of applicants pass the U.S. citizenship test.

CASE STUDY

"I applied for my naturalization in September of 2006, and of course went through the normal procedures, including the fingerprinting and the interview process. Everything went fine just took several months, and there were no unexpected difficulties. To prepare for the exam, I studied the questions for the test and discussed the process and experience with other friends that had gone through the process. I speak English, so no preparation for the English test. I studied the questions that might possibly be asked on the citizenship test and at the interview. I was sworn in on Friday July 13th. It was a very moving experience and a day I shall treasure forever. I think the ceremony was beautifully done and the judge and other people involved made it very special." —Jane

THE ENGLISH TEST

Chapter 4 discussed the naturalization interview—when people applying for citizenship meet with a USCIS officer to discuss their N-400 form. While the purpose of the interview is to ensure that the information an individual provided is accurate and truthful, the interview also serves as the first part of the English test.

Fact #189
★ ☆ ★

The speaking portion of the English test is determined
by the interview with a USCIS official.

Writing and speaking

In order for applicants to prove that they can read and write English, they must read and write sentences for the USCIS officer. Being a naturalized U.S. citizen does not require English fluency, but it does require English proficiency. Therefore, applicants do not have to read and write all of their sentences perfectly, but they must read and write at least one sentence correctly.

Fact #190
★ ☆ ★

For the writing portion of the exam, an individual will
be asked to write three sentences. At least one of the
sentences must be written correctly for the applicant
to pass the exam.

Sentences do not have to be written perfectly to count as correct; they are allowed to have errors so long as the meaning is still clear. Minor spelling, punctuation, and capitalization errors are generally OK.

The sentences that applicants are asked to read and write are not random— people learning English don't have to study every word in the language! Instead, the sentences for the naturalization test will ask about American history and government. On its website, USCIS provides a list of vocabulary words that individuals should study for the reading and writing exams.

Fact #191
★ ☆ ★

For the reading portion of the exam, an individual will
be asked to read three sentences. The applicant must
read at least one of the sentences correctly to pass
the exam.

While applicants must read at least one sentence correctly, they do not have to be perfect. According to the USCIS scoring guidelines, people can still pass the reading exam if they read without "extended pauses," read the important "content words" in the sentence, and make pronunciation errors that do not interfere with the meaning of the sentence.

THE CIVICS TEST

The civics test is conducted as an oral exam—meaning the USCIS officer asks the applicant questions, and the applicant answers verbally. To help people study for the civics test, USCIS provides a list of potential questions on its website.

Fact #192
★ ☆ ★

USCIS provides a list of 100 questions about American history and government for applicants to study.

While USCIS lists 100 potential questions for the civics test, the actual exam is much shorter—only 10 questions. USCIS can pick any of the 100 potential questions to use in a given civics test.

Fact #193
★ ☆ ★

The civics test consists of 10 questions from the USCIS list. An applicant must answer six questions correctly in order to pass.

USCIS officers are instructed to ask up to 10 questions, but to stop asking once the applicant answers six questions correctly. This means that people who answer the first six questions right only have to answer six questions total!

Most applicants should study all 100 questions, as they do not know which questions will be chosen. However, certain exemptions are made for older permanent residents who have lived in the United States for a long time. These applicants only have to study the most important questions.

Fact #194
★ ☆ ★

Applicants who are over the age of 65 and have lived in the United States for at least 20 years have to study only 20 of the 100 USCIS questions.

CASE STUDY

"I was able to become a citizen because my parents were citizens. They emigrated from Guyana in 1970, when I was a few months old. (My mother was Trinidadian by birth; my father was Guyanese. They lived in Guyana, where my father was an air traffic controller. I was actually born in Trinidad as my mother returned home for my birth— I think because I was her first child. My mother immigrated in response to recruitment efforts for registered nurses by New York City hospitals.

Since I was only seven or eight when I was naturalized, I don't remember much. I was scared walking through the halls of the immigration offices because I heard people being asked questions like, 'who's the governor of New York, who's your Senator?' I thought I was going to get in trouble because I didn't know the answer to any of those questions. I don't recall if the immigration official asked me any questions. I know I had to sign a passport-sized photo of myself—taken of me in my Catholic school uniform—which was then affixed to my naturalization certificate."

—Paulette

The test itself

The following 100 questions are the actual questions USCIS uses for the citizenship test, along with their answers. Note that, for some questions— such as "What is the name of the President of the United States now?"— the answer may change from what is listed in this book. Some questions have one precise answer, while others have multiple answer options.

1. What is the supreme law of the land?
   Answer: the Constitution

2. What does the Constitution do?
   Answers: sets up the government, defines the government, protects basic rights of Americans

3. The idea of self-government is in the first three words of the Constitution. What are these words?
   Answer: We the People

4. What is an amendment?
   Answers: a change (to the Constitution), an addition (to the Constitution)

5. What do we call the first ten amendments to the Constitution?
   Answer: the Bill of Rights

6. What is one right or freedom from the First Amendment?
   Answers: speech, religion, assembly, press, petition the government

7. How many amendments does the Constitution have?
   Answer: twenty-seven (27)

8. What did the Declaration of Independence do?
   Answers: announced our independence (from Great Britain), declared our independence (from Great Britain), said that the United States is free (from Great Britain)

9. What are two rights in the Declaration of Independence?
   Answers: life, liberty, pursuit of happiness

10. What is freedom of religion?
    Answer: You can practice any religion, or not practice a religion.

11. What is the economic system in the United States?
    Answers: capitalist economy, market economy

12. What is the "rule of law"?
    Answers: Everyone must follow the law, Leaders must obey the law,
    Government must obey the law, No one is above the law.

13. Name one branch or part of the government.
    Answers: Congress, legislative, President, executive, the courts,
    judicial

14. What stops one branch of government from becoming too
    powerful?
    Answers: checks and balances, separation of powers

15. Who is in charge of the executive branch?
    Answer: the President

16. Who makes federal laws?
    Answers: Congress, Senate and House (of Representatives), (U.S. or
    national) legislature

17. What are the two parts of the U.S. Congress?
    Answer: the Senate and House (of Representatives)

18. How many U.S. Senators are there?
    Answer: one hundred (100)

19. We elect a U.S. Senator for how many years?
    Answer: six (6)

20. Who is one of your state's U.S. Senators now?

Answers will vary. [District of Columbia residents and residents of U.S. territories should answer that D.C. (or the territory where the applicant lives) has no U.S. Senators.]

21. The House of Representatives has how many voting members?

Answer: four hundred thirty-five (435)

22. We elect a U.S. Representative for how many years?

Answer: two (2)

23. Name your U.S. Representative.

Answers will vary. [Residents of territories with nonvoting Delegates or Resident Commissioners may provide the name of that Delegate or Commissioner. Also acceptable is any statement that the territory has no (voting) Representatives in Congress.]

24. Who does a U.S. Senator represent?

Answer: all people of the state

25. Why do some states have more Representatives than other states?

Answers: (because of) the state's population, (because) they have more people, (because) some states have more people

26. We elect a President for how many years?

Answer: four (4)

27. In what month do we vote for President?

Answer: November

28. What is the name of the President of the United States now?

Answers: Donald J. Trump, Donald Trump, Trump

29. What is the name of the Vice President of the United
    States now?
    Answers: Michael R. Pence, Mike Pence, Pence

30. If the President can no longer serve, who becomes President?
    Answer: the Vice President

31. If both the President and the Vice President can no longer serve,
    who becomes President?
    Answer: the Speaker of the House

32. Who is the Commander in Chief of the military?
    Answer: the President

33. Who signs bills to become laws?
    Answer: the President

34. Who vetoes bills?
    Answer: the President

35. What does the President's Cabinet do?
    Answer: advises the President

36. What are two Cabinet-level positions?
    Answers: Secretary of Agriculture, Secretary of Commerce, Secretary
    of Defense, Secretary of Education, Secretary of Energy, Secretary
    of Health and Human Services, Secretary of Homeland Security,
    Secretary of Housing and Urban Development, Secretary of the In-
    terior, Secretary of Labor, Secretary of State, Secretary of Transpor-
    tation, Secretary of the Treasury, Secretary of Veterans Affairs,
    Attorney General, Vice President.

37. What does the judicial branch do?
    Answers: reviews laws, explains laws, resolves disputes (disagree-
    ments), decides if a law goes against the Constitution.

38. What is the highest court in the United States?

Answer: the Supreme Court

39. How many justices are on the Supreme Court?

Answer: nine (9)

40. Who is the Chief Justice of the United States now?

Answer: John Roberts (John G. Roberts, Jr.)

41. Under our Constitution, some powers belong to the federal government. What is one power of the federal government?

Answer: to print money, to declare war, to create an army, to make treaties

42. Under our Constitution, some powers belong to the states. What is one power of the states?

Answers: provide schooling and education, provide protection (police), provide safety (fire departments), give a driver's license, approve zoning and land use.

43. Who is the Governor of your state now?

Answers will vary. [District of Columbia residents should answer that D.C. does not have a Governor.]

44. What is the capital of your state?

Answers will vary. [District of Columbia residents should answer that D.C. is not a state and does not have a capital. Residents of U.S. territories should name the capital of the territory.]

45. What are the two major political parties in the United States?

Answer: Democratic and Republican

46. What is the political party of the President now?

Answer: Republican (Party)

47. What is the name of the Speaker of the House of Representatives now?
   Answers: Paul D. Ryan, (Paul) Ryan

48. There are four amendments to the Constitution about who can vote. Describe one of them.
   Answers: Citizens eighteen (18) and older (can vote); You don't have to pay (a poll tax) to vote; Any citizen can vote. (Women and men can vote); A male citizen of any race (can vote).

49. What is one responsibility that is only for United States citizens?
   Answers: serve on a jury, vote in a federal election

50. Name one right only for United States citizens.
   Answers: vote in a federal election, run for federal office

51. What are two rights of everyone living in the United States?
   Answers: freedom of expression, freedom of speech, freedom of assembly, freedom to petition the government, freedom of religion, the right to bear arms

52. What do we show loyalty to when we say the Pledge of Allegiance?
   Answers: the United States, the flag,

53. What is one promise you make when you become a United States citizen?
   Answers: give up loyalty to other countries, defend the Constitution and laws of the United States, obey the laws of the United States, serve in the U.S. military (if needed), serve (do important work for) the nation (if needed), be loyal to the United States

54. How old do citizens have to be to vote for President?
   Answer: eighteen (18) and older

55. What are two ways that Americans can participate in their democracy?
Answers: vote, join a political party, help with a campaign, join a civic group, join a community group, give an elected official your opinion on an issue, call Senators and Representatives, publicly support or oppose an issue or policy, run for office, write to a newspaper

56. When is the last day you can send in federal income tax forms?
Answer: April 15

57. When must all men register for the Selective Service?
Answers: at age eighteen (18), between eighteen (18) and twenty-six (26)

58. What is one reason colonists came to America?
Answers: freedom, political liberty, religious freedom, economic opportunity, practice their religion, escape persecution

59. Who lived in America before the Europeans arrived?
Answers: American Indians, Native Americans

60. What group of people was taken to America and sold as slaves?
Answers: Africans, people from Africa

61. Why did the colonists fight the British?
Answers: because of high taxes (taxation without representation), because the British army stayed in their houses (boarding, quartering), because they didn't have self-government

62. Who wrote the Declaration of Independence?
Answer: (Thomas) Jefferson

63. When was the Declaration of Independence adopted?
Answer: July 4, 1776

64. There were 13 original states. Name three.
Answers: New Hampshire, Massachusetts, Rhode Island, Connecticut, New York, New Jersey, Pennsylvania, Delaware, Maryland, Virginia, North Carolina, South Carolina, Georgia

65. What happened at the Constitutional Convention?
Answers: The Constitution was written; The Founding Fathers wrote the Constitution.

66. When was the Constitution written?
Answer: 1787

67. The Federalist Papers supported the passage of the U.S. Constitution. Name one of the writers.
Answers: (James) Madison, (Alexander) Hamilton, (John) Jay, Publius

68. What is one thing Benjamin Franklin is famous for?
Answers: U.S. diplomat, oldest member of the Constitutional Convention, first Postmaster General of the United States, writer of "Poor Richard's Almanac," started the first free libraries

69. Who is the "Father of Our Country"?
Answer: (George) Washington

70. Who was the first President?
Answer: (George) Washington

71. What territory did the United States buy from France in 1803?
Answers: the Louisiana Territory, Louisiana

72. Name one war fought by the United States in the 1800s.
Answers: War of 1812, Mexican-American War, Civil War, Spanish-American War

73. Name the U.S. war between the North and the South.
Answers: the Civil War, the War Between the States

74. Name one problem that led to the Civil War.
    Answers: slavery, economic reasons, states' rights

75. What was one important thing that Abraham Lincoln did?
    Answers: freed the slaves (Emancipation Proclamation), saved (or preserved) the Union, led the United States during the Civil War

76. What did the Emancipation Proclamation do?
    Answers: freed the slaves, freed slaves in the Confederacy, freed slaves in the Confederate states, freed slaves in most Southern states

77. What did Susan B. Anthony do?
    Answer: fought for women's rights, fought for civil rights

78. Name one war fought by the United States in the 1900s.
    Answer: World War I, World War II, Korean War, Vietnam War, (Persian) Gulf War

79. Who was President during World War I?
    Answer: (Woodrow) Wilson

80. Who was President during the Great Depression and World War II?
    Answer: (Franklin) Roosevelt

81. Who did the United States fight in World War II?
    Answer: Japan, Germany, and Italy

82. Before he was President, Eisenhower was a general. What war was he in?
    Answer: World War II

83. During the Cold War, what was the main concern of the United States?
    Answer: Communism

84. What movement tried to end racial discrimination?
    Answer: civil rights (movement)

85. What did Martin Luther King, Jr. do?
Answer: fought for civil rights, worked for equality for all Americans

86. What major event happened on September 11, 2001, in the United States?
Answer: Terrorists attacked the United States.

87. Name one American Indian tribe in the United States.
Answers: Cherokee, Navajo, Sioux, Chippewa, Choctaw, Pueblo, Apache, Iroquois, Creek, Blackfeet, Seminole, Cheyenne, Arawak, Shawnee, Mohegan, Huron, Oneida, Lakota, Crow, Teton, Hopi, Inuit

88. Name one of the two longest rivers in the United States.
Answers: Missouri (River), Mississippi (River)

89. What ocean is on the West Coast of the United States?
Answer: Pacific (Ocean)

90. What ocean is on the East Coast of the United States?
Answer: Atlantic (Ocean)

91. Name one U.S. territory.
Answers: Puerto Rico, U.S. Virgin Islands, American Samoa, Northern Mariana Islands, Guam

92. Name one state that borders Canada.
Answers: Maine, New Hampshire, Vermont, New York, Pennsylvania, Ohio, Michigan, Minnesota, North Dakota, Montana, Idaho, Washington, Alaska

93. Name one state that borders Mexico.
Answers: California, Arizona, New Mexico, Texas

94. What is the capital of the United States?
Answer: Washington, D.C.

95. Where is the Statue of Liberty?
    Answers: New York (Harbor), Liberty Island, New Jersey, near New York City, on the Hudson (River)

96. Why does the flag have 13 stripes?
    Answers: because there were 13 original colonies, because the stripes represent the original colonies

97. Why does the flag have 50 stars?
    Answers: because there is one star for each state, because each star represents a state, because there are 50 states

98. What is the name of the national anthem?
    Answer: The Star-Spangled Banner

99. When do we celebrate Independence Day?
    Answer: July 4

100. Name two national U.S. holidays.
    Answers: New Year's Day, Martin Luther King, Jr. Day, Presidents' Day, Memorial Day, Independence Day, Labor Day, Columbus Day, Veterans Day, Thanksgiving, Christmas

COMPLETING NATURALIZATION

After individuals pass their citizenship test, they can be sworn in as U.S. citizens. Many people remember their naturalization ceremonies as joyous days. After visas, paperwork, waiting periods and interviews, they are finally entitled to all the rights and privileges of Americans.

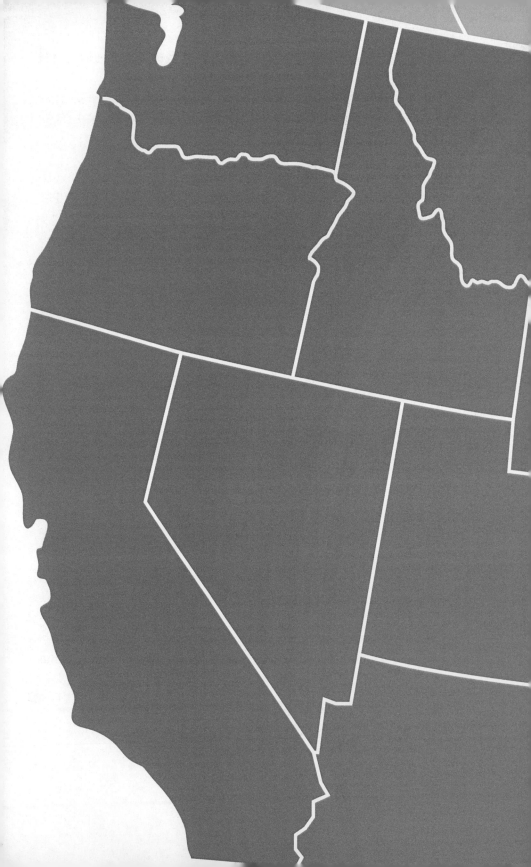

CHAPTER 10

Rights and Responsibilities of Citizenship

ecoming a U.S. citizen isn't easy. Immigrants from across the world use a variety of pathways—jobs, family connections, the lottery, and others—to gain the chance to live in the United States legally. If they are fortunate enough to become a permanent resident, they still must wait several years, become fluent in English, and learn about American culture before applying for naturalization.

Small mistakes can cost people their chance at U.S. citizenship. Individuals who have committed a crime, or lived in the United States unauthorized for any period, might be denied the chance at naturalization, and even face deportation.

Fact #195

★ ☆ ★

Over the last decade, approximately 6.6 million people have been naturalized as U.S. citizens, according to USCIS.[1]

---

1. USCIS, 2016

Despite these difficulties, hundreds of thousands of people complete the naturalization process each year. Everyone has their own reason for becoming a U.S. citizen. Some want to be able to vote. Some aspire to bring their own relatives to the country. Some hope to run for political office. Some might not have specific goals, but are feeling patriotic — like the immigrants who have come to the United States for centuries, they believe in the promise of a better life.

People choose to become citizens because being a U.S. citizen brings unique privileges. All citizens, born or naturalized, have a responsibility to uphold American values, and ensure that these privileges remain for future generations.

VOTING AND POLITICAL ENGAGEMENT

The first words of the Constitution — "We the People" — outlined from the very beginning that the American government would be run by the American people. Although a small number of elected officials are the ones who actually make government decisions, these elected officials have an obligation to fight for their constituents.

Fact #196

★ ☆ ★

Citizens earn the right to vote in state, federal, and local elections.

However, "We the People" only works if people actual vote. Unfortunately, voter turnout in the United States is typically lower than most other developed countries. Many American citizens choose not to vote — and therefore forfeit their ability to influence the country's future.

Along with the obligation to vote, citizens have the responsibility to inform themselves about political issues. Voting should not be a random guess; citizens should educate themselves about each candidate or issue before making a decision.

Fact #197

★ ☆ ★

Elections take place every year, and not just in November.

Although the president is only elected every four years, there are elections in the United States every year. Many of these elections are for local government positions, or on ballot measures that can substantially impact communities. Citizens should inform themselves about local issues and vote in the elections, too.

Voting is not the only way to be politically active. Citizens can also engage with politics by joining a political party, attending town hall meetings or protests, writing about politics, and calling their senators or representatives. All of these actions help maintain a government that is truly made up of "We the People."

CASE STUDY

"I acquired my citizenship by marriage, but still had to go through a lengthy naturalization process. The greatest benefit I have derived from being a U.S. citizen is that I get to VOTE!!! As someone who lives here, it's important to me not to be an apathetic resident. I recently published a book to thank the military men and women who afforded me this privilege. During my citizenship ceremony, the judge challenged us to do something to make a difference in our communities. I hope my book lives up to that."
— Rebecca

Jury duty

Jury duty is a special responsibility that is unique to American citizens. The Constitution guarantees that all people have the right to a fair trial. During a criminal or civil trial, the jury — and group of regular citizens — listens to both sides and delivers a verdict. Any U.S. citizen can be called upon to serve on a jury.

Fact #198

★ ☆ ★

U.S. citizens must serve jury duty when called upon.

Many people don't like serving jury duty—it requires taking a break from their regular lives, jobs, and families. Citizens can get out of jury duty, if they show that it poses a major burden for them; for example, if they would lose their job by working on the jury. Still, jury duty remains one the ways that citizens must make some sacrifice in order to uphold American principles.

Fact #199

★ ☆ ★

Individuals selected for jury duty must often take a break from their regular lives, including their jobs. However, they do get paid by the government after a few days.

Other duties

To protect American democracy, citizens must also be willing to take part in other processes of government. For example, citizens are expected to obey the laws and pay taxes on time. Male citizens are required to register for selective service, meaning that they could be required to serve in the armed forces in the event of a draft.

RESPONSIBILITIES OF CITIZENSHIP

Many of the responsibilities of U.S. citizenship are not outlined in any law. The very first immigrants—before the United States was even a country—came across the ocean seeking freedom from persecution and better lives for themselves and their families. Throughout history, different immigrant groups have likewise crossed oceans or borders seeking their own version of the American dream. Other groups, such as African-Americans and Native Americans, have likewise had to fight to be treated as equal citizens.

All citizens, whether born or naturalized, have an obligation to uphold the rights of their fellow Americans. This means respecting others, even when they come from very different backgrounds. It means recognizing that disagreement is a part of the democratic process, and learning to listen to people who think differently. And it means recognizing that these differences are not barriers, but opportunities for growth and understanding— chances to make a better country for all.

CASE STUDY

"I think that I have had a mountain of opportunities simply because I've grown up American. I grew up lower-middle class, but still, I was never subjected to the abject poverty that has plagued many Trinidadians and Guyanese. I love that I can vote and that I have the right to free speech. I especially love that the U.S. is made up of so many different types of people—I can't imagine learning about the Jewish holidays or coming to love sushi or taking Italian when I was in college if I had grown up in the Caribbean. I think that I've gained a broader worldview from being an American. And though I don't always agree with the country's leaders or with the ways in which some Americans choose to exercise their rights and freedoms, I still wouldn't trade the gleefully heterogeneous crazy mixing pot that is the U.S. for anything.   — Paulette

Conclusion

U.S. citizenship can be very simple, or very complicated. People who are born U.S. citizens don't have to think about their citizenship—they can enjoy voting, aspire to run for president, and travel the world with their U.S. passports.

People who are not born U.S. citizens face a more complicated path. They must first obtain a visa to come to the United States through one of the pathways discussed in Chapter 3. They must then follow the steps in Chapter 4 to make themselves eligible for naturalization by living as a permanent resident for at least five years. If they decide that the benefits of becoming a U.S. citizen outweigh the costs, they must make sure to learn the information in Chapters 6, 7, and 8 in order to pass the citizenship test in Chapter 9. Only after all these steps can they formally swear their allegiance to the United States and gain the full privileges of U.S. citizenship.

These privileges, of course, aren't constant. The meaning of U.S. citizenship has evolved over the course of American history. Early settlers came to North America seeking a better life; years later, some of them (and their descendants) founded a country that was governed by the people. The people have changed over time: Immigrants from across the world came to the

United States with their own hopes and dreams, but—like the original settlers—they came seeking opportunities for themselves and their families. Along the way, they brought pieces of their own cultures and values, which helped shape the country. This project is far from finished. U.S. citizens, both born and naturalized, continue to be responsible for building a nation, and defining American citizenship for the future.

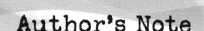

Author's Note

I was born a U.S. citizen. I know some of my ancestors emigrated from Europe (specifically Prussia and Austria) in the early 1900s; I'm not sure where the rest of my family comes from or when they gained their citizenship.

When I started college, I became friends with a lot of people who aren't U.S. citizens, and I began to realize the many was that my life was simply easier because of where I had been born. My friends and I have similar dreams, goals, and beliefs about America, but they have to deal with a lot more paperwork than I do.

Researching and writing this book helped me understand the details of citizenship and naturalization, and reminded me not to take my own U.S. citizenship for granted. I hope it has done the same for you.

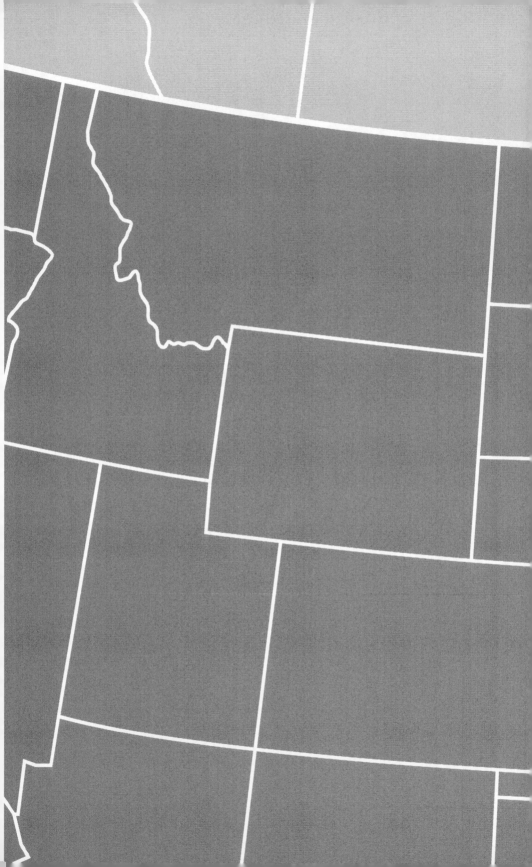

About the Author

J essica E. Piper is an American writer. She grew up in Colorado before moving to Maine for college. Some of her favorite writing topics include obscure historical happenings, contemporary social issues, and analysis of popular culture. She currently studies economics and works for a weekly college newspaper. When she is not writing, she enjoys music, travel, and spending time with friends and family.

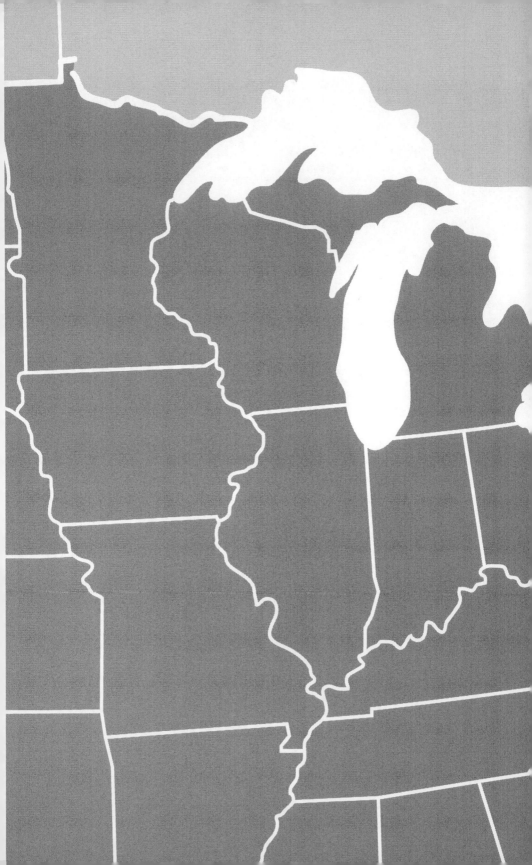

Bibliography

"Naturalization Fact Sheet." *USCIS*. USCIS, 8 Dec. 2016. Web. 17 Apr. 2017.

United States Citizenship and Immigration Services https://www.uscis.gov

United States House of Representatives http://www.house.gov

United States Senate https://www.senate.gov

Supreme Court of the United States https://www.supremecourt.gov

Library of Congress https://www.loc.gov

U.S. Department of State https://www.state.gov

Our Documents initiative https://www.ourdocuments.gov

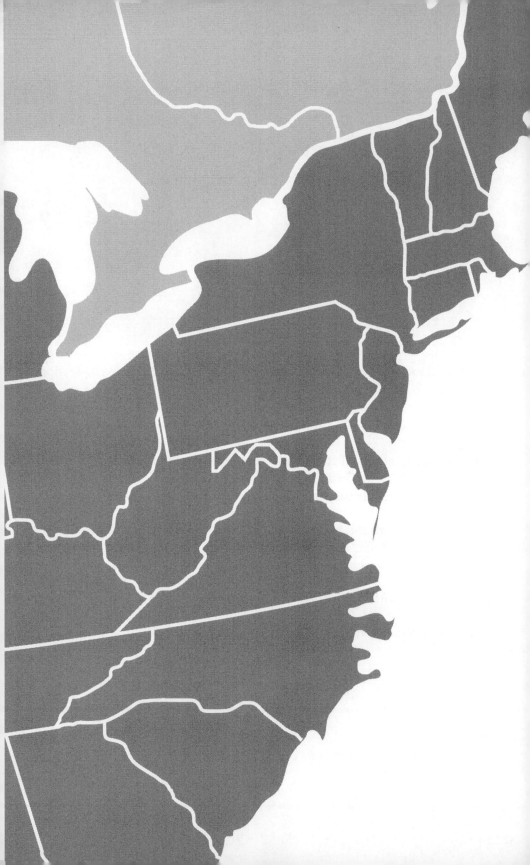

Glossary

amendment: an addition to the U.S. Constitution, for the purpose of changing or clarifying something. There have been 27 amendments to the Constitution.

14th Amendment: an amendment to the Constitution declaring — among other things — that all individuals born on U.S. soil are automatically citizens, and that all citizens deserve equal protection under American laws.

armistice: an agreement by two sides at war to stop fighting, usually in order to work out a peace agreement.

Articles of Confederation: adopted in 1777 and formally ratified in 1781, the first documents to provide a government for the United States.

asylum: legal protection granted to someone who has left their home country as a political refugee, often due to violence or persecution.

Bill of Rights: the first 10 amendments to the U.S. Constitution, ratified in 1792.

biometric: identification or statistical analysis of biological data, such as taking fingerprints.

bill: a measure introduced in U.S. Congress.

birthright citizenship: the principle that anyone born within the borders of a country is automatically a citizen.

caucus: a meeting where local members of a political party gather to pick a candidate for office.

checks and balances: a system of government where different branches of government have influence over each other in different areas, in order to ensure that no one branch obtains too much power.

Chief Justice: the judge who presides over the Supreme Court.

citizen: a legally recognized member of a particular country.

civics: the study of government and politics.

civil case: a matter brought to court because an individual's rights were violated resulting in harm; however, no law has been broken.

Civil Rights Movement: a political and social movement during the 1960s aiming to end racial inequality and achieve equal rights for African-Americans.

Civil War: a war fought between the northern and southern states from 1861 until 1865 after the southern states seceded over the issue of slavery.

constituent: a person who has the power to vote in a particular district.

Declaration of Independence: a document, signed on July 4, 1776, which proclaimed the United States to be its own country, separate from Great Britain.

Democrats: one of the two major American political parties.

deportation: removal from a country.

double jeopardy: the prosecution of the same person twice for the same crime.

draft: mandatory recruitment for military service.

dual citizen: a person who is a citizen of two countries at the same time.

Emancipation Proclamation: a declaration made by President Abraham Lincoln in 1863, which declared that all slaves in southern states were free.

entrepreneur: a person who starts a business.

enumerated powers: powers expressly listed or named. In the U.S. Constitution, the powers of Congress are enumerated in Article I, Section 8.

equal protection clause: a portion of the 14th amendment which guarantees that all citizens are entitled to the same legal privileges and protections.

Federalist Papers: a series of essays written by Alexander Hamilton, John Jay, and James Madison designed to increase popular support for the U.S. Constitution.

Founding Fathers: the individuals responsible for writing the Declaration of Independence and the Constitution.

Great Depression: a sustained economic downturn following the stock market crash in 1929.

green card: the permit which allows individuals to live and work in the United States as permanent residents.

House of Representatives: the lower chamber of the legislative branch, with 435 representatives from each state allocated based on population.

humanitarian parole: temporary permission to be in the United States issued to individuals on a case-by-case basis, usually for family or welfare-related reasons.

illegal alien: a person living in the United States without proper authorization.

income tax: a government tax directly on the money people earn from their jobs.

incumbent: the candidate in an election who is currently holding the office.

Independence Day: the holiday celebrated on July 4 each year to commemorate the signing of the Declaration of Independence.

independent voter: a voter who chooses not to align with any particular political party.

judicial independence: the separate of the judiciary from other branches of government in order to avoid political or partisan influence.

judiciary: the system of courts.

jury duty: the obligation of American citizens to serve as a juror in legal proceedings if called upon.

Korean War: a conflict between North Korea and South Korea, fought from 1950 until 1953. The United States intervened on behalf of South Korea. The war ended in an armistice, with little change in territory.

Martin Luther King, Jr.: an American minister and activist who fought for civil rights, especially equal rights for African Americans, during the 1950s and 1960s. He was shot to death in 1968.

Mexican-American War: a conflict between the United States and Mexico that began over disputed territory between the Rio Grande and Nueces River and lasted from 1846 until 1848. The United States won and acquired much of Mexico's northern territories, which would become states like California, Nevada, Arizona, and New Mexico.

naturalization: the process by which an individual becomes an American citizen.

naturalization ceremony: the final step in the naturalization process. Individuals take the Oath of Allegiance and formally become American citizens.

non-state actors: a person or organization that has substantial political influence, but is not affiliated or working with any particular government.

Oath of Allegiance: the oath individuals are required to take in order to become naturalized as U.S. citizens.

passport: a document that a country issues to its citizens, allowing them to travel to other countries.

permanent resident: an individual who lawfully possesses a green card, and therefore is allowed to live and work in the United States, regardless of their employment status.

Persian Gulf War: a conflict occurring in the Middle East following the Iraqi invasion of Kuwait in 1990. The United States led a group of United Nations forces which helped drive Iraqi forces from Kuwait.

Pledge of Allegiance: an official statement of loyalty to the United States, which was formally adopted by Congress in 1942.

poll tax: a requirement that individuals pay money in order to vote.

popular sovereignty: the principle that the power to govern a country comes from the people.

Preamble: the introduction to the U.S. Constitution, beginning with the words "We the People."

preference categories: groups that individuals are placed into based on their connections to the United States when they apply for an American visa. Higher preference categories—for individuals with stronger family connections to the United States—have shorter wait times.

president: the chief executive and highest-ranking political official of the United States.

primary elections: elections held by a political party in order to choose its candidate for the general election.

pro bono: services (such as legal advice) offered free of charge.

prohibition: a ban on the sale or purchase of alcohol, in place in the United States from 1919 until 1933.

proxy war: a conflict in which several powerful countries support different sides of a smaller conflict between other countries.

referendum: a simple yes/no vote for the general population of voters.

refugee status: a form of protection granted to individuals who face well-founded fear of persecution or other especially dangerous circumstances in their home country.

religious persecution: threat to a person's life or freedom on the basis of their religious beliefs.

Republicans: one of the two major American political parties.

Revolutionary War: a war fought by the 13 original American colonies against Great Britain in order to ensure the colonies' freedom from Britain and the establishment of the United States.

sanctions: a penalty for breaking a rule, sometimes enacted by one country on another.

selective service: a registry for men with the possibility of being drafted into the armed forces.

Senate: the upper house of the legislative branch, with 100 members—two from each state.

separation of powers: the division of responsibilities between different branches of the government in order to ensure that no one branch becomes too powerful.

Spanish-American War: a conflict between the United States and Spain in 1898. The United States won, and acquired the formerly Spanish territories of Puerto Rico, the Philippines, and Guam as a result.

Speaker of the House: the individual, usually elected by the majority part in the House of Representatives, who is responsibility for presiding over the House and setting its agenda.

Star-Spangled Banner: the national anthem on the United States, written as a poem by Francis Scott Key in 1814.

Statue of Liberty: the statue of a woman holding a torch, located on Liberty Island in New York Harbor. The statue is often thought to symbolize freedom and democracy.

suffrage: the right of women to vote.

suffragists: individuals who fought for women's voting rights.

supremacy clause: Article VI, Clause 2 of the U.S. Constitution, which establishes that the Constitution is the supreme law of the land, and that federal laws overrule state ones.

Supreme Court: the highest court of the United States, responsible for determining the constitutionality of laws.

Temporary Protected Status: an assignment that allows individuals to be granted temporary visas in the United States because of dangerous conditions in their home country, such as a natural disaster.

term limit: a restriction on the number of consecutive terms for which an elected official can run for office.

unconstitutional: a law—local, state, or federal—that is found to violate the principles of the Constitution, and is therefore void.

undocumented immigrants: people residing in the United States without proper authorization.

veto: the power of a president to reject a law passed by Congress. However, Congress can override a presidential veto if two-thirds of members in both houses vote to do so.

Vietnam War: a conflict fought in Southeast Asia between the 1950s and 1970s. North Vietnam, which was communist, invaded South Vietnam. The United States intervened on behalf of South Vietnam, but ultimately pulled out of the war. North Vietnam achieved victory in 1976.

visa: a document granting individuals the legal right to live, work, or visit the United States.

War of 1812: a conflict between the United States and Great Britain, which—despite its name—lasted several years. A peace treaty was signed in 1814, but the two sides continued fighting until 1815.

work authorization: the right to work for pay in the United States.

World War I: a European conflict which erupted in 1914 after a Serbian rebel shot an Austrian archduke. The United States joined on the side of the Allied Powers (led by Britain and France) in 1917, and the Allies won in 1918.

World War II: a global conflict primarily which began in 1938 and was fought between the Axis Powers (Germany, Japan, and Italy) and the Allied Powers (Britain, France, Russia, and the United States). The Allies achieved victory in 1945.

Index